A WORLD OF DIFFERENCE
THE BIG GREEN POETRY MACHINE

Southern Poets

Edited by Lisa Adlam

First published in Great Britain in 2009 by:

 Young**Writers**

Young Writers
Remus House
Coltsfoot Drive
Peterborough
PE2 9JX
Telephone: 01733 890066
Website: www.youngwriters.co.uk

Foreword

Young Writers' A World of Difference is a showcase for our nation's most brilliant young poets to share their thoughts, hopes and fears for the planet they call home.

Young Writers was established in 1990 to nurture creativity in our children and young adults, to give them an interest in poetry and an outlet to express themselves. Seeing their work in print will encourage them to keep writing as they grow, and become our poets of tomorrow.

Selecting the poems has been challenging and immensely rewarding. The effort and imagination invested by these young writers makes their poems a pleasure to enjoy reading time and time again.

Contents

Barnwood Park Arts College, Gloucester

Izabelle Butler (12) 1
Zoe Hollt (12).. 2
Elizabeth Isaac (12) 3
Holly Stokes-Ewers (12)........................ 4
Maria Donna Aylmer (11) 4
Beth Chandler (12) 5
Holly Fleur Gillingham (11) 5
Naomi Adams (13)................................... 6
Jessica Louise Watson (11).................... 6
Katie Jones (11) 7
Nicola Bircher (11) 7
April Bailey (13) 8
Christy Barnett (11) 8
Jennifer Hill (12) 9
Deanna Payne (11) 9
Aishah Panchbhaya (12)...................... 10
Natasha Horton (12).............................. 10
Joanna Wells (12) 11
Alice Hughes (11) 11
Stephanie Say (12) 12
Rachel Ellen Dewhurst (11)................... 12
Ishrat Fadra (11)..................................... 13
Vienna Satchwell Monet (11)................. 13
Niamh Ritchie (11) 14
Olivia Moon (11)..................................... 14
Leanne Beechey (11)............................. 15
Georgina Haines (12) 15
Danielle Spencer (13) 16
Ella Jakeway (12) 16
Camilla England (12).............................. 17
Kirsty Rosie (11)..................................... 17
Casey James (11) 18
Flora Jane Rougvie (11) 18
Sarah Anna Milne (11).......................... 19
Martha Atkinson (12) 19
Charlotte Clissold (12) 20
Georgina Emily Ashman (11) 20
Lucy Hobbs (12)..................................... 21
Vikkie Hambling (14) 21
Ellysha Williams (12)............................. 22

Jess Hollyhead (14)................................ 22
Georgie Newcombe (12)......................... 23
Nicole Riddick (12), Daisy Goddard &
Sydney Ann Weir.................................... 23
Renae Mia Wilson (11)........................... 24
Leah Ellis (11).. 24
Jasmine Sarah Peters (11).................... 25
Emma Dunn (12)..................................... 25
Eleanor Maynard (11)............................. 26
Charlie Brobyn (11) 26
Rianne Adamson (12)............................. 27
Ranelle Norman (12).............................. 27
Hannah Maughan (11)............................. 28
Hollie Smith (12)..................................... 28
Morganne Charlotte Yates (11)............. 29
Elle Holmes (11)..................................... 29
Molly Finnegan (12)................................ 30
Laura-Elizabeth Murphy (14)................ 30
Sophie Alice Miller (11) 31
Lucy Ann Humphreys (11) 31
Sophie Jenkins (11)................................ 32
Jessica-Jo Griffiths (13) 32
Sharmaine Stanley (11) 33
Chloe Wattam (12)................................. 33
Ellie Mitchell (13)................................... 34
Eleanor Tuckfield (12) 34
Holly Winfield (12)................................. 35
Rosanna Harris (11) 35
Alice McMaster (14) 36
Courtney King (11) 36
Isabel Nicole Barnett (11)...................... 36
Robyn Biggs (11) 37
Danielle-Marie Powell-Chakkori (11)... 37
Asma Bibi Moosa (13)............................ 37
Jessie Taylor (11) 38

Cantell Maths & Computing College, Southampton

Jamie Jacobs (14) 38
Mohammod Sufian (11)......................... 39
Katie Fisher (11)..................................... 39
Joe Maund (12) 40

Isabel Cockarill (11) 40
Sehar Nosrati (11) 41

Cardinal Hinsley Maths & Computing College, London

Neil Fernandes (13) 41
Tiago Lopes-Caires (13) 42
Shane Baines (13) 43
Ebuka Ene (13) 43
David Ocran (13) 44
Anton Lewis (12) 44
Glodie Ifura (13) 45
Matheus Henrique Souza (13) 45
Santiago Figueroa (14) 46
Alie Bittar (13) 46
Mustafa Assadi (13) 47
Isaiah Oji (13) 47
Benedict Ifura (11) 48
Shermarl Ricardo Hay (12) 48
Luis Jose Silva Valente (12) 49
Aron Fezzehaie (13) 49
Tobi Amao (13) 49
Julius Vidad (11) 50
Dennis Ward (11) 50
James Kearney (11) 50
Tosin Banjo (13) 51

Chalfonts Community College, Chalfont St Peter

Kayleigh-Anne Georgia Gibson (12) 51
Josh Gill (11) 53
Lois Walley (11) 53
Ben Whitbread (11) 54
Elizabeth Whiting (11) 54
Emma Chitty (11) 55
Zach Nelmes 55
Marium Ladha (11) 56
Sam Mills (12) 56
Zara Glaister (12) 56
Katie Brooks (11) 57
Rebecca Hickman (12) 57
Halima Osman (12) 57
Maeve Higgs 58
Jack Dalston (11) 58

Chipping Campden School, Gloucester

Edward Edgerton (11) 58
Rebecca Bonham (11) 59
Carys Harmer (11) 59
Becky Knight (11) 60
Toby Wheeler (11) 60
Daniel Wookey (11) 61
Charis Warnock (11) 61
Tom Purchase-Rathbone (11) 62
Kayleigh Drewitt (13) 62
George Seymour (11) 63
Lauren Foster (12) 63
Chloe Masters (11) 64
Maddie Higgins (11) 64
James Bartoli-Edwards (11) 65
Sabrina Rew (11) 65
Jordan Mazzina (11) 66
Tyler Megan Barnett (11) 66
Elliott Routh (11) 67
Charlotte Creed (11) 67
Robbie Faulkner (11) 68
Andrea Latham (11) 68
Grace Dembowicz (11) 68
Beatrice Saxon (11) 69
Matilda Willson (11) 69
Bethany Ellen Walker (11) 69
Jac Johnson-Fisher (11) 70
Verity Copeland (11) 70
Daniel Mallinson (11) 70
Aaron Evans (12) 71
Aaron Smith (12) 71
Tom Price (11) 71

Coloma Convent Girls' School, Croydon

Jessica Hughes (12) 72
Rachel Akinsanya (11) 73
Sandra Ofili (11) 74
Sophie Jones (12) 75
Hannah Morley (12) 76
Rocio Crispin (12) 77
Emelia Drury (11) 77
Claudia Merlini (13) 78
Hannah Foley (11) 78
Molly McGing (12) 79
Niamh Ingram (12) 80
Francesca Pereira (11) 81

Nicole Bowler (11) 82
Julia Rooke (11) 83
Rebecca Humphreys (12) 84
Megan Hammond (12) 84
Heather Lafferty (12) 85
Georgia O'Sullivan (11) 85
Oma-Louise Odigboh (12) 86
Maria Nelligan (12) 86
Emily Quartly (11) 87
Laura Brophy (12) 87
Elizabeth Crilly (12) 88
Charlene Coutinho (12) 88
Anna Garcia (11) 89
Katie Ross (13) 89
Louise McPheat (12) 90
Emily Findlay (11) 90
Charlotte-Nicole Mamedy (12) 91
Stephanie Adaken-Garjah (11) 91
Rachel Limb (12) 92
Ella Fernandes-Pinto (11) 92
Jessica Brennan (12) 93
Claire Ward (11) 94
Maria Hickland (12) 95
Hannah Pepper (13) 96
Alessia Marcovecchio (12) 97
Jenny Roberts (12) 97

The Angmering School, Angmering

Sophie Isaacs 98
Emily Catling (12) 99
Aicha Rakhdoune, Stuart Howman
& Emma Calder (13) 100
Harriet Colmer (12) 101
Kerry Jennings (12) 101
Emily Tester (12) 102
Chloe Booker 102
Rebecca Collier (13) 103
Amber Bryant & Jorjia Nye (12) 103
Jodie Adams 104
Charlotte Podesta (13) 104
Claire Heberlein (12) 105
Jazmine Loricci (12) 105
Adam Mowbray, Lily Parisi (12) &
Tara Moynihan (13) 106
James Collins 106
Matthew Livett (12) 107

Tom Jenner 107
Stefan Coney (12) 108
Adele Sami (12) 108
Holly Coomber 109
Alex Jones (12) 109

The John Bentley School, Calne

Jordi James Green, Cory & Daniel
Spyer 110
Kerry Flynn (11) 111
Paige Warren (11) 111
Jordan Cleverley (14) 112
Corrinne Young (11) 112
Olivia Lauren Mackay (12) 113
Stacey Webster 113
Elliot James Snudden (11) 114
Marc Matthews (13) 114

**The John of Gaunt School,
Trowbridge**

Emily (12) 114
James Ivory (12) 115
Rosie Brewer (13) 116
Aimee Ashworth (12) 116
Rose Vinnicombe (13) 117
Annabel Wood (12) 117
Carla Rookley (12) 118
Crystal Morgan (12) 118
Olivia Tetik (12) 119
Ben Pocock (12) 119
Lucy Newton (12) 120
Adele Houkes (12) 120
Beth Jones (12) 121
Stephanie Hall (12) 121
Shante Nash (12) 122
Michael Hoare (12) 122
Michala Blake (12) 123
Megan Jones (12) 123
Manja Suffian-Warr (12) 124
Lauren Fox (12) 124
Nathan Hulbert (12) 125
Jemma Houkes (12) 125
Amber Coward (13) 126
Sam Horsley (13) 126
Rebecca Dewfall (13) 127
Scott Pullen (12) 127
Dan Phillips (13) 127

The Poems

Help Me!

The world is dying
Under our feet
Swept away like a pebble in the sea
So help me! Help me!

Pollution and CO_2
Destroying the atmosphere
As if it was a speck of dust
That is not right
So help me! Help me!

Destroying the rainforest
Habitats too
The trees screaming as they're cut down
Poor animals
So help me! Help me!

The world is dying
And we are killing it
As if it was not important
So help me! Help me!

Help me save the world
Help me!
Please help me! Please
Help me!

Izabelle Butler (12)
Barnwood Park Arts College, Gloucester

1

Make Every Day A Special Day

Make every day a special day,
Children laughing and no one has to pray,
Rainforest stands up tall,
Homeless people have houses with walls,
If only this were true.
Make every day a special day,
Children laughing and no one has to pray,
No child had to ring 999
And everything would just be fine,
If only this were true.
Make every day a special day,
Children laughing and no one has to pray,
Guns are gone, there are no wars
And pollution is no more,
If only this were true.

Make every day a special day,
Children laughing and no one has to pray,
There would be no difference from black and white,
Or anything in-between,
Everyone would work together,
It would be a big, worldwide team,
If only this were true.

Make every day a special day,
Children laughing and no one has to pray,
My poem could go on forever,
But no one has the time,
I hope you read and understand the reason
Why I wrote this rhyme,
Help me make this true!

Zoe Hollt (12)
Barnwood Park Arts College, Gloucester

I Am A Lonely Hermit

Here I stand,
Tall and straight,
Anchored deep underground.
Here I am, a lonely hermit,
Stuck up on this hill.

Looking down upon the town,
It is a sorry sight,
I don't know how you breathe,
Because of all the fumes,
Coming from the cars and factories,
Why can't you walk and save us all?
Public transport, ride a bike,
All the possibilities!

Out of the corner of my eye,
To all my fellow trees, bye-bye,
Deforestation - that's what it is,
Why don't you buy recycled?
For I could be next,
Recycle all your bottles,
Your tins, cans and clothes,
Empty the landfill sites,
Don't litter, please!

You're destroying our environment,
Burning up our atmosphere,
Why, oh why, oh why?
You could kill us all,
For I am a lonely hermit,
Standing tall, yet sad.

Elizabeth Isaac (12)
Barnwood Park Arts College, Gloucester

Do You Know?

Think of all the animals that have lost their homes,
Due to deforestation to the world they've known,
What are they going to do?
Where are they going to go?
Do you know?

Think of all the people that haven't got a home,
We need a house machine that makes lots of clones,
What are they going to do?
Where are they going to go?
Do you know?

Think of all the glaciers that are melting down,
All this business is giving us frowns,
What are we going to do?
How are we going to help?
Do you know?

Think of this world that is full of war,
It is really now becoming a real bore,
How are we going to stop it?
We've got to hop to it!

Think of all the litter that is on the ground,
It is becoming a real mound,
As soon as we make it disappear,
It will just reappear.

Now stand up and be seen,
Everybody be green!

Holly Stokes-Ewers (12)
Barnwood Park Arts College, Gloucester

Do Your Bit!

Burning fossil fuels doesn't help at all,
Landfill sites filling up right until they're full,
Many people do recycle, but not quite enough,
Global warming getting higher, this could be quite tough,
Now you see my point of view, let's make it into action!

Maria Donna Aylmer (11)
Barnwood Park Arts College, Gloucester

4

If I Could Change The World, I Would

Here is my rhyme
To stop pollution and crime
Global warming has to stop
Cos one day this world will go pop!
Floating, flying, this world is a dream
But we don't realise
We just wake up and beam
Stabbing to kill is no way
To get stress out
Cos you will always pay
I would love to live in a world
With eco-friendly cars
No cruelty
No deforestation
Clear skies to see the stars
No more drugs
Means no more thugs
If you turn off lights
You'll be able to afford flights
If you're cold, turn to woollies
And don't respect those
Who are bullies
Don't be a murderer
Or do something wrong
And don't be a burglar
That's the point of this song!

Beth Chandler (12)
Barnwood Park Arts College, Gloucester

Dear World, Get Well Soon

The environment is dying
The government is lying
Who is to blame?
For this world, it's a shame
Make peace, not heat
Be clean, go green!

Holly Fleur Gillingham (11)
Barnwood Park Arts College, Gloucester

5

Our Vast World?

The vast world has gone
No one is moving
No one is talking
This is not like before
All full of joy and fun
And now just despair

My friends have gone
The cold is harsh and unforgiving
Eyes wide with death
This is not like before
Friends ecstatic, future coming
And now it is no more

The water is still
Dreams have faded
A world has been lost
Not like before
The hustle and bustle
A new land of hope
And now it is melting away

All classes are the same
Awaiting, light and darkness
We cannot remember before
Only that sound, that noise, that fear
For those who are no longer with us.

Naomi Adams (13)
Barnwood Park Arts College, Gloucester

Recycle

R eady to be green?
E nergy to be saved!
C ompost helps your plants
Y our fruit; you'll be amazed!
C ars give off fumes
L andfills are filling up
E nvironmentally friendly - we mustn't give this up!

Jessica Louise Watson (11)
Barnwood Park Arts College, Gloucester

Litterbug

Look at all the litter,
Oh, what can we do?
It's on the ground,
In the pond,
Even on my shoe!

Look at all the litter,
It really isn't nice,
It's crawling with insects
And attracting lots of mice!

Look at all the litter,
It really is obscene,
What we're doing to our Earth,
Is very, very mean!

Look at all the litter,
It really isn't fair,
The way we treat our planet,
But no one seems to care!

Where has all the litter gone?
It's somehow disappeared,
Somebody has cleaned it up,
To them we give three cheers!

Katie Jones (11)
Barnwood Park Arts College, Gloucester

Being Green

Recycling and being green,
Is one way of being clean,
Metal, paper, plastic, glass,
Any amount, any mass,
The landfill sites are full of rubbish,
The world will be gone,
The world we should cherish,
Cleaning up this world is great,
Hurry up, before it's too late!

Nicola Bircher (11)
Barnwood Park Arts College, Gloucester

Do You Know Where I Am?

Do you know where I am?
The trees are whistling in the breeze
The ants are crawling up my knees
The streams are crashing against the rocks
The ants have just crawled down my socks.

Do you know where I am?
The saws are hacking at the bark
Then it leaves a mark in my heart
I feel them suffering to their deaths
They will have no more breaths.

Do you know where I am?
The gorillas have no more homes
Soon they will be just a pile of bones
The bugs are crying with disappointment
Killing the trees will kill their excitement.

Do you know where I am?
If you could see the pain I see
You would come and help me
Save the rainforest
Because there may be none left!

Think about it!

April Bailey (13)
Barnwood Park Arts College, Gloucester

The Animals

I was watching the news
When something made me cry
Oh, why do people not know
About the animals that die?
And soon they will be extinct
Oh why, oh why, do we hurt them
When they haven't done anything wrong?
Can't you see they have a right on Earth?
They are living things just like us.

Christy Barnett (11)
Barnwood Park Arts College, Gloucester

A Second Chance

What would you do
If you could start anew?
Would you change your ways
To try and save
The animals from extinction
The world from pollution?
All the lovely things are dying
Our world is slowly frying
All the diseases
Some people it pleases
Religions like Hinduism
Don't agree with vandalism
But people are choosing
To start overusing
All this talk about global warming
It should be a warning
People don't understand
That we are killing the land
But you should fight
To get things right
And start to save our world
We are destroying!

Jennifer Hill (12)
Barnwood Park Arts College, Gloucester

Space Monster

Right up in the universe,
Lives a monster with a curse,
All the planets with no care,
He'd guzzle like a grizzly bear.

And because this world's undoubtedly next,
To be swallowed by the monstrous hex,
Put your can in the green bin,
Then we won't be in,
(And this really isn't funny)
His giant, fat, hairy tummy.

Deanna Payne (11)
Barnwood Park Arts College, Gloucester

A Better Place

Help make the world a better place
To put a smile on everyone's face
Make this world free from attacks
Children cry, but no one reacts

Help make the world a better place
To put a smile on everyone's face
Make all the bad people disappear
So no single person has to fear

Help make the world a better place
To put a smile on everyone's face
No killing, no drugs, no child abuse
Children and adults, both getting confused

Help make the world a better place
To put a smile on everyone's face
No littering, no pollution, no being mean
Be good, be kind, be nice, be green

Help make the world a better place
To put a smile on everyone's face
No animal cruelty, feed the ducks in the pond
So this world will be better for our children to live on.

Aishah Panchbhaya (12)
Barnwood Park Arts College, Gloucester

Animal Court

This world is a terrible place for animals
There is rubbish shooting through the world like cannonballs
It needs to be cleaned up
So this is enough
I will have to go; it's killing us

People are careless, no one ever cares
Everything always ends in despair
We will have to do it ourselves, no doubt
We want out
Now!

Natasha Horton (12)
Barnwood Park Arts College, Gloucester

Saving The World Today

S ave the world
A s you go along
V iolence and war
I s to be stopped
N o lights left on
G reener world for all

T rees are dying
H ere and all around
E nding this green world

W orld is fading into dark
O ur fault mostly
I nstead of driving
R un and walk
L eave the car behind
D on't leave all the green

T oday help the world
O ur world is crashing down
D o all the things that you think of
A ll the ways you can
Y ou need to help save our world.

Joanna Wells (12)
Barnwood Park Arts College, Gloucester

Save Our Planet

E nergy saving
N o littering
V ery little recycling
I nappropriate dumping
R educe waste
O ur resources are in danger of being misused
N ever throw away what you can recycle
M ake our planet a better place
E nvironment should be protected
N ot too late to save our planet
T ry better to look after our world.

Alice Hughes (11)
Barnwood Park Arts College, Gloucester

Save Our Planet

Pollution, make it stop,
Chopping trees, gases, vandalism, the lot!
Our world is dying,
While we are frying
And pollution,
Is caused by driving.
Litter and graffiti and also disease,
It really does not please,
Polluting and overusing,
Is very overwhelming,
Landfill is bad,
It makes people sad.
Do not drive your cars,
But go on your bikes,
Or even walk,
Or go for a hike.
Global warming is killing homes,
Which would you rather? Home or contaminated dome?
Our world is dying,
While we are frying,
Save our planet!

Stephanie Say (12)
Barnwood Park Arts College, Gloucester

Write World!

W hen the world began, years before today
R unning in an extremely clean way
I remember when cars came
T hen those big aeroplanes
E veryone thought it was great
   But left the world in a terrible state

W e will clear the world
O f course, pollution will be hurled
R euse the mess you make
L ove what is at stake
D o something today!

Rachel Ellen Dewhurst (11)
Barnwood Park Arts College, Gloucester

Environment Issues

Litter, cars, gas and fuels
It's all well known, like some kinda jewels
We say nothing will happen
But we'll all know when global warming shows.

Fossil fuels are burnin'
Landfill sites are turnin'
Carbon monoxide carries on churnin'
All this making global warming
So listen up, here's the warnin'!

Rubbish, recycling is the tool
Then landfill sites will stop with their gruel
Which I have to say, would be cool!

Cars, aeroplanes, everything with fuel
What do you think? I'm some kinda fool?
But carbon monoxide even ruins a pool!

So everybody, here we go
A few little reasons to help you know
What damage is being done to the world
So save our planet, save us all!

Ishrat Fadra (11)
Barnwood Park Arts College, Gloucester

Recycle

Recycling, recycling, recycling is good
Make sure you do it
It will do the world some good.

I know you can't be bothered
But just put it in the bin
You never know, it could become another thing.

Don't pollute the world
Don't throw garden waste
Just take it to the tip
And make the environment a pretty and better place.

Vienna Satchwell Monet (11)
Barnwood Park Arts College, Gloucester

Our Earth

Its life is buried in our minds
The sun, the air, the spirit
The enchanting colours of the world
No one knows how much we'll miss it

The elements of nature destroyed by CO_2
Although we cannot see it
It's destroying me and you

A toddler taking its first steps
A boy climbing his first tree
A newborn taking its first breath
For the first time I can see

The sweet breeze lifting me off my feet
The paths guiding my mind
The sun trailing away
Yet there is nothing new to find

The handprints of our nature
No longer are they free
Lying beneath the damage
Soon, you will see.

Niamh Ritchie (11)
Barnwood Park Arts College, Gloucester

Our World

Our world is a dump
In a bag
Full of bumps

The rubbish in our rivers
Crying with tears
So recycle your beers

But if we work hard
We can recycle our card
Put things right
In our own backyard.

Olivia Moon (11)
Barnwood Park Arts College, Gloucester

About Climate Change And Flooding

Too much rain
Too many storms
Even more flooding
In our world

Even more homes ruined
Even more buildings ruined
More money to repair
Feel so sorry for people who care

Poor polar bears in the Arctic
And poor penguins as well
Poor walruses, they will get affected
Poor animals, no ice for them to catch their prey
Or rest and there are lots more animals too

So, when someone tries to make a joke
About climate change or flooding or something like that
Don't laugh, don't giggle
It's not a laughing or giggling matter
The world is getting ruined
I don't think it's funny . . . do you?

Leanne Beechey (11)
Barnwood Park Arts College, Gloucester

Definitely No More

Here is my rhyme
To stop pollution and crime,
Be green - turn off lights
And definitely no more fights
If you're cold, don't turn on heating
Just wear woollies
And definitely no more bullies
I hate it when I hear about murders
And definitely no more burglars
I want to live in a world with eco-friendly cars
No vandalism, child abuse
Clean skies to see the stars!

Georgina Haines (12)
Barnwood Park Arts College, Gloucester

Animals And Extinction

Animals are dying
Poachers are defying
They lay their traps
To catch big cats
They lay in pain
For Man to gain
It's such a shame
They are so lame!

Soon, they'll all be gone
If we don't stop them doing wrong
Animals' homes are being destroyed
It makes me feel so annoyed!
Seals are getting hunted down
While others begin to frown
Pandas are rare
Does anyone care?
Gorillas protect their territory
While hunters hunt aggressively.

Danielle Spencer (13)
Barnwood Park Arts College, Gloucester

The World Could Be A Better Place

The world could be a better place
So there would be a smile on every face
Start with something like pollution
Try to find a solution
Then move on to global warming
In the Arctic, ice needs to start forming
Hunting should be banned, in my point of view
Or the animal population will be few
Stop using all these cars
Or I will move straight to Mars
People should stop smoking
Because when I walk in town, I start choking
Once you have finished this huge operation
I will live in a better nation!

Ella Jakeway (12)
Barnwood Park Arts College, Gloucester

We Have Opposites Unfortunately

Here is my poem,
To stop homelessness and poverty.
I don't know about you,
But I don't think about it every day.
But when I do,
I'm shocked.
Just think of all the things we have
And the people who have nothing.
We have toys and books and food,
They don't.
They have starvation, poverty and drought,
We don't.
By 'they', I mean the homeless,
The poor,
The people that we walk past and fear,
The people on the floor.
We shouldn't have to write poems like this,
But we have opposites unfortunately . . .

Camilla England (12)
Barnwood Park Arts College, Gloucester

The Litter Poem

Don't litter!
Because it's killing our planet.
Recycle instead,
To save our seabed.
We're killing the fish, whales and seals,
Because of our car wheels.
Going round and round, making gases,
We're killing the planet in masses.
Our animals are dying out in this world,
Our tigers and elephants will never be heard.
So save up your bottles, tins and jars
And stop using your cars,
To go to places you can walk to in no time
And that's the end of my save the world rhyme!

Kirsty Rosie (11)
Barnwood Park Arts College, Gloucester

17

Reuse, Reduce, Recycle

R euse, reduce, recycle
   This is what we should be thinking
E nvironmentally friendly waste disposal
   Not heaps of landfill sites sat there stinking
C arbon dioxide and greenhouse gases
   Cause global warming and climate change
Y ou can and should do your bit
   The environment will repay you in exchange
C onsistently thinking of ways
   To save the Earth as we know it
L ater on, your children will be glad
   That you did it
I ce caps are melting
   Due to global warming
N o more filling up the bin
   You've had your warning
G o and start recycling today
   Reuse, reduce, recycle, not throw it away!

Casey James (11)
Barnwood Park Arts College, Gloucester

Climate Change

C onstantly people are destroying the Earth
L ittle hope remains of saving the world
I magine a world without any life
M illions of animals, plants and people will die
A ll because of us
T errible losses of life will occur
E ach day, the world is being destroyed

C louds of doom envelop the Earth
H oping that something will save us from the great peril ahead
A ll we have left, our hearts and souls
N ow we must act, before it's too late
G athering together, we can prevent this fate
E verybody act now, before time runs out!

Flora Jane Rougvie (11)
Barnwood Park Arts College, Gloucester

A Bag For Life . . .

Pollution is in the seas,
Pollution is in the air,
Help all we can,
Be aware and care.

Recycle and reuse,
Where we can,
All work as a team,
So it all goes to plan.

Aerosols are harmful,
They break the ozone down,
We need to stop spraying,
To save our cities and towns.

We need to reduce our rubbish,
To stop landfill sites,
They are taking over the world,
So use a bag for life!

Sarah Anna Milne (11)
Barnwood Park Arts College, Gloucester

Endangered

Bang!
A tiger is shot dead in the head
The hunter doesn't care that it's dead
Bang!
The tigers are not supposed to be dead
But the hunter can't get this through his head
Bang!
The giant panda's life has been cut short
But the hunter doesn't give it a second thought
Bang!
Loads of animals are endangered
But they are still murdered
Bang!
So, please give shooting another thought
Before another animal's life is cut short.

Martha Atkinson (12)
Barnwood Park Arts College, Gloucester

Take A Look Around!

Have you ever stopped and stared,
To take a look around?
The Earth is getting destroyed by us,
Above and underground.

I know people are always moaning,
'Everyone's turning green,'
Trees are getting cut down more and more,
Not an animal to be seen.

Wasted electricity,
Cutting down the trees,
Running short on money,
Rising taxes and seas.

But have you ever wondered,
What's causing all this pain?
Let's try and solve these problems
And make the world smile again.

Charlotte Clissold (12)
Barnwood Park Arts College, Gloucester

Save The Planet

Litter all around,
Litter on the ground,
Dropping litter is not good,
Always do what you should,
Don't drop litter anywhere,
There are plenty of bins around here and there,
There's litter everywhere,
You should take a lot of care,
Rubbish on the ground
Can also fly around,
Every day litter is thrown away,
But not in a bin,
Right under your chin,
Littering is bad for the environment and you,
Don't drop litter or it will affect you.

Georgina Emily Ashman (11)
Barnwood Park Arts College, Gloucester

Our Special Place

Our planet is a special place,
Please don't think to vandalise,
Please work hard to keep it clean,
We'll be grateful if you did.

Don't use cars and trains and planes,
Don't use guns and bombs and tanks,
Don't kill trees and plants and cubs,
We'll be grateful if you don't.

Please scrub hard on walls and windows,
Please ride bikes to stop pollution,
Please put guns down, stop the fighting,
Please have bins for the rubbish.

Our planet is a special place,
Please don't think to vandalise,
Please work hard to keep it clean,
We'll be grateful if you did.

Lucy Hobbs (12)
Barnwood Park Arts College, Gloucester

Dear Mr And Mrs World!

Dear Mr and Mrs World,
I'm writing this apology,
To show you how I feel,
How driving cars and hairspray cans,
Make this world surreal,
The sea levels are rising
And floods are taking over,
New technology and advertising,
The fuel in your Land Rover,
Hurricanes, tornados, the ice caps are melting,
Forest fires, dried-out land and hailstones pelting,
I hope you forgive me,
As I know I have done wrong,
I look around me and I see,
Devastation and destruction that went on for so long.

Vikkie Hambling (14)
Barnwood Park Arts College, Gloucester

21

Change!

If we survive this weather crisis and lack of heat
I wonder what we're supposed to eat
But the ice is melting in the North
Leaving the polar bears to flee
As we sit here and do as we please
Trees stand there in the forest, looking glum
Knowing that their time will come
I understand your point of view
And what people have spread around
But people are using boats and rafts to get around
The government don't seem to really care
They send their men to strip the planet bare
I won't change my opinion
They can warn me all they want
The time is now, choose another path
You have a choice, stand up and be counted
For whatever happens, make it time to rejoice!

Ellysha Williams (12)
Barnwood Park Arts College, Gloucester

We Are Sorry

Sorry for chopping your trees down
And for making you frown
Sorry for making your land flood
And for drying out your mud

Sorry for making the sea levels rise
Why don't we stop and think about our demise?
Sorry for causing fires and making the forests burn
Why don't we ever learn?

Sorry for all the whirling tornados
That we are actually killing you, no one knows
Sorry for all the damaging hurricanes
And for all the fumes coming from the planes

Sorry for melting most of your ice
From now on, I promise, we will be nice!

Jess Hollyhead (14)
Barnwood Park Arts College, Gloucester

Save Our World

Vandalising,
Overusing,
Polluting
And waste,
It takes up too much space!
We need to save our land,
So everyone stand, lend a hand,
Don't chop down trees,
Stop the litter, please,
Recycle what you've got,
Cardboard, plastic, the lot,
Walk or ride a bike,
Use less gas,
Don't take the car,
Stop this riot,
Then it will be more quiet,
Save our land!

Georgie Newcombe (12)
Barnwood Park Arts College, Gloucester

Save Our Planet

P is for pollution, make it stop
O is for overusing, please don't drop
L is for landfill, it needs to stop smelling
L is for litter, it's very repelling
U is for Uranus, it's cleaner than Earth
T is for trees, you need them on your turf
I   is for insulation, keeping your house warm
O is for online, buy a mower for your lawn
N is for new, save our world from turning into goo!

Pollution! Make it stop!
Pollution! Please don't chop!
Pollution! Down our trees!
Pollution! Please! Please! Please!

Nicole Riddick (12), Daisy Goddard & Sydney-Ann Weir
Barnwood Park Arts College, Gloucester

I Am A Polar Bear . . .

Fish are dying, food gone scarce,
What am I supposed to do?
My cubs are hungry, I am too
What shall I do?
What can I do?
How can I feed us all?
Oh!

I've lost little Berry on a melting iceberg,
What about the others?
I can't have it happening again.

I'm so confused, what's happening to the Earth?
Why is it so hot?
Why is my family dying?
Am I going to be the last of my kind?
Somebody help me!
Please!

Renae Mia Wilson (11)
Barnwood Park Arts College, Gloucester

Everyone Should Recycle!

R ecycle, recycle, please help
E veryone give a big yelp
C ars, aeroplanes, when they came
Y es, the world was dirty again
C lean, clean up our world, you don't even have to pay
L etting animals live again, woo-hoo! Yay!
E at anything that came out of a tin or plastic

P lease, please help, because it's fantastic
L ive in a clean way from now
E veryone will say, 'Wow'
A t this time, we say, 'Hello,' to a bus
S ing along and dance with us
E veryone come and join in with us!

Leah Ellis (11)
Barnwood Park Arts College, Gloucester

When I Go Outside . . .

When I go outside, I see rubbish on the floor,
I think, what a waste, what about all those poor?
Why don't people put their rubbish into bins?
Some animals won't be here for our next of kin.

When I go outside, I see so many lights,
I think, we're losing our sun, the world won't be so bright!
More gases in our air,
It's killing our home, does anyone even care?

When I go outside, I don't see recycling places,
I think, soon enough the world will be full, rubbish will cover everyone's faces
I gave myself a fright,
When I went to the landfill site,
We need to save our Earth, OK?
We need to save it today!

Jasmine Sarah Peters (11)
Barnwood Park Arts College, Gloucester

Why?

Why do we have poverty?
Why do we have pollution?
Why do we have racism?
Why do we have wars?
These are all the things
I need answers to,
So why don't I have answers now?

Litter is everywhere,
Disease is everywhere,
Why do we have these things?
I love this world and so should you,
Then why is it still a mess?

I know what we need,
We need it now,
So why isn't it here yet?

Emma Dunn (12)
Barnwood Park Arts College, Gloucester

Eco-Friendly

E is for the environment that we must preserve
C is for the conservation of the rainforests
O is for the ozone layer that we are destroying

F is for the forest renewal
R is for the rubbish that we throw on the floor
I is for the infra-red radiation that is warming up our planet
E is for the energy saving light bulbs that reduce carbon emissions
N is for the nuclear power plants that might have to provide our
energy in the future
D is for the devastation of the planet caused by carbon dioxide
L is for the landfill sites that release harmful gases
Y is for the young people that may never get old, because of the
effects of carbon dioxide.

Eleanor Maynard (11)
Barnwood Park Arts College, Gloucester

The World Is

The world is like
An ancient Spanish galleon
She needs someone to attend the wood

The world is like
A demanding newborn infant
It needs to be loved

The world is like
A sparkling diamond ring
It's small and beautiful

The world is wonderful
And bright, wild and fragile
Will we lose it in a little while?

Charlie Brobyn (11)
Barnwood Park Arts College, Gloucester

26

Tomorrow May Never Come

Look around you, what is happening to the world?
The last thing I remember . . . I was just a little girl . . .
The grass was green and the trees were big
The animals and the rainforests were the 'in' thing

But now, pollution, war and crime
Are taking up everyone's time
Death, violence and global warming
Is filling the world with vermin

We might think the world is OK
We might just be here for today
But tomorrow, the world might have gone away
Then what will you say?

Rianne Adamson (12)
Barnwood Park Arts College, Gloucester

We Are Finished

Recycle, recycle, everywhere
Think about all of the polar bears
Litter, litter, on the floor
Chewing gum, chewing gum, on the wall.

Just take a rest from driving around
Just listen to the sound of the ground
Is that cracking?
No, it's the sound of litter dropping.

Think of what the world would be like if it were clean
So has everybody seen?
We would love to have a clean planet
So try and please, keep it clean.

Ranelle Norman (12)
Barnwood Park Arts College, Gloucester

We Have

We have fields, then they are littered,
We have rivers, then they are polluted,
There are adverts and websites to tell us to stop this,
But does everyone listen? What is the solution to pollution?

What happens if the forests are gone away?
Do we let it happen another day?
And floods happen from global warming,
That is a big warning to stop what we are doing.

We will recycle our cans; recycle our paper,
We can just do the best we can.
Pass down clothes, shop for only what we need
And soon the environment and us, will be smiling with glee.

Hannah Maughan (11)
Barnwood Park Arts College, Gloucester

Save Our Planet

Diseases spreading fast
The three Rs, let's hope they last
Global warming to greenhouse gases
The landfill that is massive.

Do not vandalise
Just look and realise
Save the animals from being extinct
Or the world will be gone before you've blinked!

It will all be gone soon
The sun and the moon
The animals and stars
So bye-bye Earth, hello Mars!

Hollie Smith (12)
Barnwood Park Arts College, Gloucester

Shout Out!

On a Tuesday, in our road,
It's green box collection, so I'm told,
We do our bit to save the planet,
Climate change, I wish we could ban it.

Litterbugs, they drive me crazy,
They really are very lazy,
No thought, no care, they're not aware,
The harm they do, it's just not fair.

If every human would stop and think,
To see how much we are on the brink,
A little bit goes a long way,
If we keep on saving, we can shout, 'Hooray!'

Morganne Charlotte Yates (11)
Barnwood Park Arts College, Gloucester

Recycling

Recycle your bottles
Recycle your cans
You just don't know
They could become frying pans

Recycle your garden waste
Recycle your metal
So that the world's flowers
Can have pretty petals

Recycle your clothes
Recycle your shoes
Because there's lots
Of things you will lose.

Elle Holmes (11)
Barnwood Park Arts College, Gloucester

Our Environment

Recycle cans, recycle tins,
Reduce the waste in our bins.

Car fumes, bus fumes, fumes everywhere,
Destroying the ozone layer
And people don't seem to care.

Carrier bags are all manmade,
They become a pest, because they don't degrade,
They choke our fish and harm our birds,
All this, because of thoughtless nerds.

We can all think of ways to keep the air clean,
Because the time has come to start thinking green!

Molly Finnegan (12)
Barnwood Park Arts College, Gloucester

Dear World, What Have We Done?

Dear world,

All the things we've put you through
It's hard to believe it's something we'd do
With dry land and flooded
Where is this world headed?

Can we stop this problem now?
With scientists to show us how
You're not gone, the cure is here
No more need to fear.

With all the things we've put you through
It's time to change, for me and you.

Laura-Elizabeth Murphy (14)
Barnwood Park Arts College, Gloucester

I Hear You Say

I hear you say,
Trees, who needs them?
I hear you say,
Recycling, who needs it?
I hear you say,
Green space, who needs that?
You hear me say,
Trees, we need them!
Recycling, we need it!
Green space, we need that!
You hear me say,
Our environment, it needs us!

Sophie Alice Miller (11)
Barnwood Park Arts College, Gloucester

Tree-Cycle

Imagine if you were a tree,
Happy and free,
Under the bright sun,
Animals surround you, having fun.
Out of nowhere comes a deafening roar,
You look back, at a great beast standing there.
The animals flee, fearing their homes will be destroyed,
But you, the tree, cannot move.
You stay there, in front of the great beast that's laid before you,
The beast gets closer . . . and closer,
Until it has gone past, leaving a trail of twigs where you were.
Save the tree . . . recycle!

Lucy Ann Humphreys (11)
Barnwood Park Arts College, Gloucester

My Very Own Poem

I hate the fact that the animals are becoming extinct
I know it is us making them die
So when I think about it, I start to cry
Please don't litter
You're destroying our world
It is not just your world
Other people have to live here too
Everything is up to you
Please don't litter
Why hunt? It's horrible and the animals you kill
They haven't done anything wrong
So why hunt?

Sophie Jenkins (11)
Barnwood Park Arts College, Gloucester

Litter

When I walk down the street
I feel so surrounded by a river of litter
More like a sea of rubbish
Just like the Red Sea
Full of different colours and movements

At school, girls dropping litter
Like raindrops
Begging flies and rats
To visit

Why bother having bins?

Jessica-Jo Griffiths (13)
Barnwood Park Arts College, Gloucester

Untitled

Hearing about animals becoming extinct
Makes me really think
All the icebergs are melting
And I know we are not helping
We can help by not using cars so much
This will do the finishing touch
Everyone could walk a little journey
So the animals don't all die
Come on, you have got to try
Please don't let all the animals become extinct.

Sharmaine Stanley (11)
Barnwood Park Arts College, Gloucester

The World

The smell of petrol when I walk down the street,
The sight of the homeless in the city,
The sound of people arguing in the street,
The world is getting worse, every day,
Why are we so mean to the Earth?
The sight of people being bullied and no one doing anything about it,
The sound of people being racist to others,
The smell of people smoking drugs, as they walk past,
What is the world coming to?
We should look after the planet we're on!

Chloe Wattam (12)
Barnwood Park Arts College, Gloucester

Rainforest

R ainforest, rainforest
A nimals are in danger
I nsects and other bugs becoming extinct
N ot a good idea for our plants
F stands for forest
O ur population in the forest is getting terrible
R ainforest, rainforest
E asy to
S top polluting the rainforest
T oday, recycle paper.

Ellie Mitchell (13)
Barnwood Park Arts College, Gloucester

Destroying The World

Before, I didn't realise,
I thought everything was dramatised,
Every time I turn on the lights,
Away melts some more ice,
Every day crime roams the streets
And pollution flows through the streams,
Deforestation
And extinction,
Working together,
Destroying the world!

Eleanor Tuckfield (12)
Barnwood Park Arts College, Gloucester

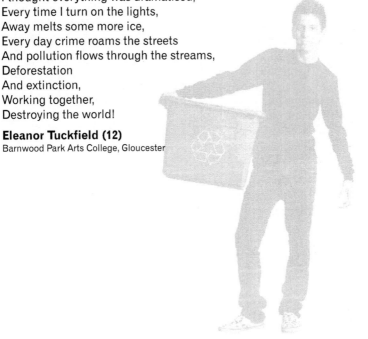

Save Our Planet!

We are killing the planet,
Just as we speak,
To save the planet, we could recycle, reduce, reuse.

We are hurting the world,
Just as we speak,
To save our world, we could not litter, not drive, not waste.

We are spoiling the Earth,
Just as we speak,
To save the Earth, we could walk, cycle, stop cutting down trees.

Holly Winfield (12)
Barnwood Park Arts College, Gloucester

Care For The World

All around us is unclean air
Because you cannot see it
You forget it's there

Global warming, pollution
These are some things
With solutions!

Do your bit
We're in a race
To make the world a better place!

Rosanna Harris (11)
Barnwood Park Arts College, Gloucester

Pollution

P is for poverty, it makes you poor
O is for one species of animal
L is for littering, polluting the world
L is for lovely people that save the world
U is for understanding different races
T is for tramps looking for food
I is for it's about time people made a difference
O is for one, two, three; rainforests are no more
N is for never understanding how to recycle.

Alice McMaster (14)
Barnwood Park Arts College, Gloucester

Drop No Rubbish

Drop no rubbish,
Make no mess,
Make the world not look a mess,
Drop your rubbish,
If you like,
Just think of the wildlife you are killing,
Animals need their homes,
Animals are like us, they need a home and food,
So why drop rubbish on their home?

Courtney King (11)
Barnwood Park Arts College, Gloucester

Plants

P ollution is destroying our planet
L andfill sites are getting too full
A ct right now, or we could die
N ow the rainforests are being cut down
T rees help give us oxygen
S now could disappear if we don't help the environment.

Isabel Nicole Barnett (11)
Barnwood Park Arts College, Gloucester

The Environment

Our landfill sites are overfull,
They just can't take anymore,
They give off a smell which is not nice,
So we've got to help to stop all the rats and mice.

We don't throw all our rubbish away,
We recycle now, to help in every way,
Cans, paper, cardboard too,
Recycle all these for a better place for me and you.

Robyn Biggs (11)
Barnwood Park Arts College, Gloucester

Pollution

This world we live in, is not as green
Not as green as it might have been
With cars and trains, boats and planes
They all participate in the bosses' gains
The cows on our planet, eating grass
It makes them produce methane gas
Aerosols, cartons and packaging too
Should make us think about what we do!

Danielle-Marie Powell-Chakkori (11)
Barnwood Park Arts College, Gloucester

Pollution!

Everywhere I go, I see black smoke everywhere,
Little animals choking on the smoke and dying,
Cutting down beautiful trees, leaving animals homeless and hungry,
Climate changing and causing global warming,
Litter, litter, everywhere, most of it can be recycled,
So recycle 'cause it's part of your life cycle,
If you don't recycle, you will be able to taste your own waste,
If this doesn't stop, it will get worse and this world will burst!

Asma Bibi Moosa (13)
Barnwood Park Arts College, Gloucester

Pollution, Pollution

Pollution is in the air
Pollution is on the ground
Just stop pollution everywhere

The birds cannot fly
The fish cannot swim
They animals cannot breathe
Are we all going to die?

Jessie Taylor (11)
Barnwood Park Arts College, Gloucester

Recycled

I walked through the busy street
I saw a bunch of litter under my feet
In the bin was
A metal tin
In the park was an empty bottle of gin
But in the pond was a floating tin

On the way, driving to work
In my battered Merc
I was driving so fast
Unfortunately, I ran over a piece of glass

The tyre went bang!
I had a prang

I had to walk through a busy street
Now I am not looking very neat
Fit for the bin
My broken tin

My green, broken car
Will be recycled to go far.

Jamie Jacobs (14)
Cantell Maths & Computing College, Southampton

38

Litter Problems

L itter all around us.
I nternational problems which
T ogether we can solve.
T ime is going quickly,
E ach person must do their part.
R ound the world.

P ut your rubbish in the bin.
R esolve this growing problem.
O ur Earth will be gone
B efore we even know it.
L et's all work together
E ven the children
M ake our world a better place.

Mohammod Sufian (11)
Cantell Maths & Computing College, Southampton

Climate Change

C hanging the world to a better place
L itter is the thing that we have to face
I think we all need to pull together
M aking the world good forever
A frica is badly in need of help
T ime to let out the critical yelp
E xtinction is happening before our eyes

C hallenge ourselves to save the future
H ate to not go on the computer
A lways remember not to litter
N ever be able to see the weather bitter
G lobal warming needs to stop
E veryone can do something to save our world.

Katie Fisher (11)
Cantell Maths & Computing College, Southampton

Think Green!

We need to protect our environment,
Because it's what we need to survive,
Animals are hunted and killed every day,
We don't want them extinct, just alive.

Nature is taking a beating,
Storms and flooding year after year,
Weather is so unpredictable,
It's caused by global warming I fear.

Pollution is killing our islands,
The sky, the air and the sea,
If we don't try to save our planet,
They'll be nothing, no you nor me.

Joe Maund (12)
Cantell Maths & Computing College, Southampton

Environment

I don't want the world to end
Because the environment is my friend
Trees are dying
So I am crying
Oh no, acid rain is coming again
I now go inside my trusty den
I think of all the fish dying out there
Then I think it's not fair!

Isabel Cockarill (11)
Cantell Maths & Computing College, Southampton

Pollution!

Pollution, what a terrible thing
Pollution, makes the world sing
For a solution to stop pollution
Pollution needs to be minimised
The people around the world
Should open their eyes
Don't wait for it to get worse
The ozone is about to burst!

Sehar Nosrati (11)
Cantell Maths & Computing College, Southampton

The Earth

I have a green, beautiful garden,
I love my garden,
I water it every day,
The next day, it dies away,
I used to get fruit and flowers from my plants
But now I get yellow, falling leaves.

My 'place of clear water'
Where springs washed into the shiny grass
But now I see muddy patches
Before I used to see clear sky
But now I see dark smoke
Like I have been in a world of evil.

Stop destroying my Earth
I won't destroy your life
Look after me and I will look after you.

You stole my forest
I will steal your everything!
You lie on the grass in summer
You lie in the bed in winter
If you don't have grass in summer
Then you don't have a place to lie.

Neil Fernandes (13)
Cardinal Hinsley Maths & Computing College, London

Gun Crime - Haikus

People under the
Age of eighteen being shot
Shot dead on the streets.

Breaking the records
A new year, a new record
Because of stabbing.

Innocent people
Caught up in the wrong place
At the worst time ever.

Lots of young children
Bringing knives and guns to their
Homes, schools and the streets.

Saying they're going
To stab or shoot you if you
Don't give them your things.

But they have to learn
One thing when they kill someone
They'll be arrested.

But when they try to
Rob a gang member, they could
End up being dead.

So, before you say
A prayer, just think about those
Who have lost loved ones.

Tiago Lopes-Caires (13)
Cardinal Hinsley Maths & Computing College, London

Green Generation

Green generation,
Learn about that,
The world is dying,
Along with my pet cat.

Animals, plants and people too,
It's all happening,
With so much we can do.

We must work together,
Make everything right,
With all as one,
We can defend and fight.

We don't have a lot of time,
To make the world OK,
But with what we can do,
We can make it a happy day.

A happy day,
A happy year,
Even a happy life,
Show we have no fear.

Shane Baines (13)
Cardinal Hinsley Maths & Computing College, London

Global Warming

Why won't people stop?
Our grandchildren may not see exotic animals
And they won't be able to grow crops
The poisonous gases polluting the air
We can hardly breathe
Without the fear of inhaling this toxic waste
It's ruining the world
Like a monster eating up the human race
The quick change of weather
Destroying and terrorising the hopes
Of our little boys and girls.

Ebuka Ene (13)
Cardinal Hinsley Maths & Computing College, London

Everyday Global Warming

I climbed the mighty mountains,
Just to see them crumble.
I admire nature's luscious forests,
Only to see them cut and burnt down the next day.
I advance through the blizzard and snow
And I am greeted by melting ice.
I wake up to sunlight,
Soon to be shrouded by grey clouds:
As I walk to work,
I see houses destroyed by hurricanes and tornados.
Today I'm having my house refurbished,
As a flood occurred at night, due to a rise in sea levels.
I saw the polar ice caps,
Polar bears were swimming in the ice-cold water,
That's all there was, no land, just water.
Global warming happens every day,
So now we must right our wrongs
And be part of the green generation.

David Ocran (13)
Cardinal Hinsley Maths & Computing College, London

Is It Us?

The world needs help,
The animals need help,
The Antarctic needs help,
But do we need help?
We, as humans, have our own minds,
But what stops us from getting behind?
Is it us, badly behaving?
Is it you, continuously talking?
We need to put this to an end!
Help the world! The world needs you
And there may be a surprise for you!
We act different, we think different,
We talk different!
But yet, we are all the same!

Anton Lewis (12)
Cardinal Hinsley Maths & Computing College, London

Why Does It Have To Be?

Why does it have to be?
My children's children won't see polar bears
We can't breathe, all we see is fading away
They say the future is bright
But are they talking about Earth?
Because if we carry on
Nothing would be spared
The countries just blame each other
Except for helping one
They cut down trees
Like there is nothing wrong
Can't they stop
I say let's finish this off
Stop the pollution
That's the solution.

Glodie Ifura (13)
Cardinal Hinsley Maths & Computing College, London

Tsunami

I'm tsunami . . .
I'm caused by you
By your pollution, deforestation
I'm tsunami . . .
I'm warning you
If you don't stop hurting the forest
I'm going to attack, attack and attack again
If you help me, I can help you
I'm tsunami . . .
You are destroying nature
I will destroy your houses, buildings
Everything
Just stop hurting me.

Matheus Henrique Souza (13)
Cardinal Hinsley Maths & Computing College, London

Working Together

Working together
We can make the world better
If we work as one
I am sure we can go further up
The Earth is going down
While we are thinking
That we are doing the right things
Trees, flowers and rivers are drying out
While we are trying to figure it out
The atmosphere, it's breaking up
The clouds are blowing away
The blue sky turning to black
While we are smoking and who knows what else

Santiago Figueroa (14)
Cardinal Hinsley Maths & Computing College, London

Earth Is Dying

Pollution is killing the planet
Which means our home is dying
We need a plan
So we can save our future

Every one of us are killers
So you need to stop and think
All it takes is to turn off the light
Then everything will be alright

One day it will be fine
But till that day
We need to help
So just think about what you are doing.

Alie Bittar (13)
Cardinal Hinsley Maths & Computing College, London

46

Earth

I am tired, every second, every minute,
Every hour, every day, every week, month, year, century.
I hear an excuse from you,
I am trying to convince you of extinction,
But you will not agree.
I am trying to convince you to recycle,
But you ignore me.
I told you about pollution and how to stop it,
But you ignored me,
I had nothing more to tell you,
So I gave up,
You won't listen.

Mustafa Assadi (13)
Cardinal Hinsley Maths & Computing College, London

Global Warming

Global warming, what have they done?
Will I live to see the first birthday of my son?
Why did they do this, thinking only of themselves?
Not thinking what effect it will later have on the world
Pollution from factories, oil tanker spillages
Burning down rainforests, destroying villages
They call us the green generation
We have to unite every colour, religion and nation
Protests, campaigns, petitions, the lot
To cut down global warming and put it to a stop
Global warming, what have they done?
Will I live to see the first birthday of my son?

Isaiah Oji (13)
Cardinal Hinsley Maths & Computing College, London

Wasteland

The penguin population is going down
The ozone layer is breaking down
The temperature is getting hotter
And the ice is melting now
The Earth is shrinking into the gutter
The atmosphere is crawling up
Now the control in our hands is slipping like butter
Trees are falling, even bears
Soon the Earth will turn to thin air
We don't look after the world, because we don't care
Because our planet is going to blow!

Benedict Ifura (11)
Cardinal Hinsley Maths & Computing College, London

Pollutions And Smoke

Global warming is bad for us,
Carbon monoxide comes out of a double-decker bus,
It must stop now, or we cannot survive,
People have got to walk, instead of drive.

Every day cars and trains are here,
This is a problem that everyone fears,
The Earth is starting to smell bad,
Pollution is starting to add and add.

The Earth is getting small and small
And trees and bushes are starting to fall.

Shermarl Ricardo Hay (12)
Cardinal Hinsley Maths & Computing College, London

Will I Survive?

I was made by a big bang
By the clap of a hand
Once, I was beautiful
But now I'm suffering
I give them beauty
But they give me pollution
I'm dying because of them
Will they care for me?
Will I survive?
No one knows.

Luis Jose Silva Valente (12)
Cardinal Hinsley Maths & Computing College, London

You Don't Care About Earth

I care about you, but you don't care about me,
Only yourselves.
I am melting and animals are dying,
The Earth is sad, but you're happy,
The Earth was peaceful, but you destroyed it,
By fighting each other and starting wars.
I put you in a safe place, but you put yourself in danger,
By destroying that place,
I am in danger, but you don't care.

Aron Fezzehaie (13)
Cardinal Hinsley Maths & Computing College, London

Environmental

Burning heat surrounds us all
We cause damage to the environment, if you didn't know
But there's much to do, still a chance, to save the world
Recycling and reducing your carbon footprint can help, you know
Litter scatters to the floor
Recycling a can a day will help the most . . .

Tobi Amao (13)
Cardinal Hinsley Maths & Computing College, London

Global Warming

Polar bears are dying
Because the heat is rising
This is because of global warming
Try your best to recycle
And then the Earth will stop dying
The Earth is frying
Animals are crying
Population wouldn't grow
Instead it would shrink very low.

Julius Vidad (11)
Cardinal Hinsley Maths & Computing College, London

Survive

The Earth is dying,
The sea is crying,
Try to recycle,
Use a bicycle,
The Earth is shrinking,
The ice is melting,
Global warming is bad,
The Earth is very sad.

Dennis Ward (11)
Cardinal Hinsley Maths & Computing College, London

Global Warming

Global warming is so bad,
It makes me very sad,
We wouldn't waste a single tree,
It makes me very angry,
Don't use wood, instead use turf,
Then you'll start to save the Earth,
Little bits by a time,
Recycle or commit a crime!

James Kearney (11)
Cardinal Hinsley Maths & Computing College, London

The Polar Bear

A polar bear is really white
If it finds food it can be met
With a very big bite
A polar bear lives on ice
It's really cold and nice
Global warming is really bad
It makes the bear seem really sad.

Tosin Banjo (13)
Cardinal Hinsley Maths & Computing College, London

Animals

Poor little animals
All around us
Hedgehogs and monkeys
Why don't you care?

Let's be fair
Put junk in a bin
Then all those
Animals keep their hair!

All this rubbish
Kills them all
Try not to smoke
But instead have a joke!

Now you know
What to show
So let's be fair
And let's keep our hair!

Kayleigh-Anne Georgia Gibson (12)
Chalfonts Community College, Chalfont St Peter

The Colours Of The Earth

Black, white and brown
Different colours
Same world
The Earth is
A trap waiting
To be snapped
At any innocent
Person willing
To take a risk
And enter it.
Different colours cover
The Earth.
These colours cause
Death, humiliation, threats and hatred.
As the Earth stands still
There is movement all
Over the Earth.
The Earth is made
Up of two types
Of people.
The right
And the wrong.
Why is it that
The colours
Of the Earth
Bring and cause
Unwanted suffering?
Why do innocent
People have
To be treated
Like this?
Why is it that
The colours of the
Earth cause wars that
Are not needed?
What if there were hoards of people
The same colour
And only one person different?

This person
This one person . . .
Why does he have to

Be humiliated
Because he is different
From the others?
Maybe it's the way he dresses?
Maybe it's the size of him?
Maybe it's because he
Is not as wealthy as
The others . . . ?
Or maybe it's jealousy . . . ?
Ask yourself this
Why does
This person have to be
Humiliated
Because he is different?
Why does the Earth cause and
Bring unwanted suffering?

Josh Gill (11)
Chalfonts Community College, Chalfont St Peter

Going . . . Going . . .?

Tigers are my favourite,
But they are becoming rare,
It's because of so many things,
Why don't some people care?

They're hunted down so easily,
Their jungles are being torn down,
Cruel people skin their fur,
Then sell them in a small town!

It's not just tigers,
It's pandas too
And lots of other animals,
Some are taken captive and they haul them to the zoo!

Some people do care,
It's not just me,
Others though,
Need to stop and see!

Lois Walley (11)
Chalfonts Community College, Chalfont St Peter

Homelessness

The homeless are so poor
They are also lonely
They are everywhere
They must be very sad
Some may not have a mum or a dad

They do not have homes
They could be very thin
When they were young
They were not looked after properly
Or they could have been kicked out

They all have no friends
They probably have never washed
They stink of mud
Some die young
And some die old.

Ben Whitbread (11)
Chalfonts Community College, Chalfont St Peter

Endangered Animals

Animals are everywhere you go,
They die with an arrow and a bow,
We kill them every day,
By the pollution that we make.

We kill them by using cars,
Running over their tails,
Hedgehogs, wolves, foxes and sheep,
Is what is going to be extinct!

We need to stop killing them,
With guns and poison which hunters use
And bonfires that we do,
So think and stop killing!

Elizabeth Whiting (11)
Chalfonts Community College, Chalfont St Peter

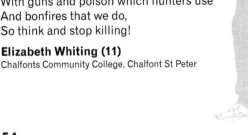

Homelessness

People live in dustbins, people live in boxes,
But everyone who is homeless has to fight foxes,
Some bins are big, yet some bins are small,
But poor old homeless people have to eat from them all!

Some people beg, some people smoke,
But don't smoke too much, or you will just choke!
Every homeless girl or boy is as loving as a flower,
Pretty as an eagle, but oh, very sour!

So there is my poem, very wise and real,
Everybody give the homeless people money,
Because you made a deal!

Emma Chitty (11)
Chalfonts Community College, Chalfont St Peter

Rainforests

R ainfall is so high
A nother bird in the sky
I t is so big
N othing is so amazing
F orest but bigger
O ur jungle
R ain is their sun
E nough trees
S nakes every place you look
T allest trees you will see
S ee it, then you believe it.

Zach Nelmes
Chalfonts Community College, Chalfont St Peter

Rainforest

R aucous sounds amongst the trees
A pleasant hum of bumblebees
I s there such a place anywhere else?
N othing can match the beauty and its wealth
F or God has created this blessing to treasure
O h, if we destroy it, we extinguish our pleasure
R ainforest, oh rainforest, your splendour is divine
E verlasting you should be, your exquisiteness should shine
S mell the aromatic blooming flowers
T he rainforest will amuse you, for hours.

Marium Ladha (11)
Chalfonts Community College, Chalfont St Peter

Pollution

P eople use cars
O ver miles and miles
L oads of fuel
L oads of CO_2
U ses up too much atmosphere
T otally destroys
I ncluding wildlife
O f course, it kills everything
N ever again shall it happen!

Sam Mills (12)
Chalfonts Community College, Chalfont St Peter

War

W ar is bad, it makes me sad
A nd people who die, make other people cry
R emember those who helped us during that painful moment
And remember we should all be friends
And not be one another's opponent!

Zara Glaister (12)
Chalfonts Community College, Chalfont St Peter

Recycling

R educe, reuse, recycle
E nvironment
C ardboard
Y ou can recycle to help save the planet
C ans
L iving your life to recycle
I t helps trees to live
N ever throw away anything that can be recycled
G reen!

Katie Brooks (11)
Chalfonts Community College, Chalfont St Peter

Recycling

R unning around
E verywhere in the
C ar park
Y ou yawn, getting tired
C ollecting up any bottles and cans
L aunching it in
I know
N othing can stop me now
G reater place for you and me!

Rebecca Hickman (12)
Chalfonts Community College, Chalfont St Peter

Poverty All Around Our World

P eople need help
O nly you can help them
V ery serious
E verlasting memories
R emember those less fortunate
T ry to give to charities
Y ou can make the difference in people's lives.

Halima Osman (12)
Chalfonts Community College, Chalfont St Peter

Pollution And Global Warming

People keep creating pollution,
By driving their cars,
Going on the bus is a simple solution,
Recycling paper, tins and jars,
Can help forests and trees,
We are creating the greenhouse effect,
Don't kill animals, especially bees,
Please help, before our world is wrecked!

Maeve Higgs
Chalfonts Community College, Chalfont St Peter

Poverty

P oor and have no money
O uch! It hurts sleeping on the pavement
V ery sad
E very penny counts
R eally, I wish I had money
T o spend on a proper dinner
Y et tonight, it's soup again.

Jack Dalston (11)
Chalfonts Community College, Chalfont St Peter

The War Poem

Guns being fired from trench to trench,
Lives being lost every day,
Wars go on - years on end,
Bombs hitting innocent people,
Tanks roaring through deserted villages,
Where people left for their own safety,
Grenades being thrown,
Blood spurting from people's heads.
Suddenly, all is quiet -
As wars end, happiness comes back to planet Earth.

Edward Edgerton (11)
Chipping Campden School, Gloucester

58

Bad World

Has the world really come to this?
Pollution, destroying the rainforests and being racist,
Let me tell you, if you think death and starvation are cool,
There are others out there that have no food
And cannot go to school,
All the treats and desires we have,
When others can only starve,
Life is unfair and the world is mean,
But at least we can help it by being green,
Recycling cardboard, plastic and cans,
Can help the air and acres of land,
From everything to everyone,
Is this what the world has become?
The world is good, but Man is not,
From the elephants he kills, to the flies that we squat,
But I'm telling you now, this must stop!
I'm telling you now that this must be changed,
The world must be better and Man rearranged,
For every life has value, you see,
From a human being to a bug or a tree,
That's why we must stop killing, being racist and polluting
And begin being fair, saving the world and the life that is living,
Because I'm sure we would all like to see the world a better place,
For me and for you and for all the human race,
Because in the future what is not to be heard,
Is that this planet of ours, is a bad world!

Rebecca Bonham (11)
Chipping Campden School, Gloucester

We Can Help - Haikus

We are destroying
Millions of animals
But we can help it

I wrote a haiku
About changing the climate
Because we can help.

Carys Harmer (11)
Chipping Campden School, Gloucester

59

Think!

Once upon a time, there was a world that shared
And a world that appreciated,
People were at peace with others,
Harmony was shared among every continent known to Man,
It didn't matter what language they spoke
Or what colour their skin,
The world had a plan that it would stay like this forever,
But it didn't.
People began to fight and wars would overcome
Villages would be destroyed
And there would be nothing left but ash.
Is this the world we started with?
Or have we destroyed it with our careless mistakes?
We should learn how to accept the consequences of our actions,
Hundreds of people die every day from hunger and thirst
And even pollution intoxicating their lungs.
So just think of what we are doing to the world
And the people in it
And just think, are we the ones to blame for this despicable truth?
Who could call this a perfect world
When nothing is perfect at all, not even close,
So what will become of us and our precious world?
I can't help but wonder, in many years to come,
Will there be any such thing?

Becky Knight (11)
Chipping Campden School, Gloucester

Trees And Oxygen

As the day goes through and through
People don't care what they do
They cut down trees as much as they please
And don't have any respect for you.

All the time they cut them down
But what about oxygen?
They cut them down by the ton
Leading to animals who have gone.

Toby Wheeler (11)
Chipping Campden School, Gloucester

War Life

The smell of man's sweat
A sight of shattered men
Sound of gunfire
And the taste of blood

Why is there war?
It is like déjà vu every day for us
A distant cry every heartbeat
We want to go home

I am wounded
He is dead
It's an awful sight
But a very often one

Every now and then
A gun round erupts
We turn, blood all over the ground
It is not right

Why is the world like this?
Why did we join the army?
Somebody stop this
If only they knew how we feel.

Daniel Wookey (11)
Chipping Campden School, Gloucester

The Barren And Lifeless Land

You'll be sad that you didn't help
When all the animals have been made extinct
Because we destroyed their habitats!
Imagine a world without lights and electricity
Without animals and pets
Without food and drink
And you have to walk on the hard and bare, barren land
And that's what will happen if you don't act now
So start helping now
And the world will live a long and happy life!

Charis Warnock (11)
Chipping Campden School, Gloucester

Global Warming

The world is changing
And not for the better,
Global warming,
Is taking over.

The ice caps are melting,
Polar bears are dying,
The weather is changing,
High winds and flooding.

It's time for us to do our bit,
Walk or bike to school if you can,
This will cut down pollution,
Pick up your litter off the floor
And put it in a bin.

Don't leave your TV on standby,
Always turn it off,
Recycle all your rubbish,
Well done, you've done your bit!

Tom Purchase-Rathbone (11)
Chipping Campden School, Gloucester

Recycle Waste

Recycle your waste
For better taste.

Beware of the fox
In your black recycling box
Because when you throw a tin in
It might make a din
Recycle your waste
For better taste.

So when you mow the lawn
Be ready for dawn
Because your green bin
Will go for a spin!

Kayleigh Drewitt (13)
Chipping Campden School, Gloucester

The Perfect World

In a perfect world
There would be no more
Gangs, armies and wars.

I wish no one made guns,
Or no one had bad thoughts,
About knives and they were used
Purely for their purpose.

I wish no one thought of
Force as strength
And strength as power.

The world was a nice place
Without thoughts of war
Guns and armies
With nothing but happy, clean thought.

No more violence!

George Seymour (11)
Chipping Campden School, Gloucester

Recycling

Bottles, bags and tins too
You can recycle them,
'Come on! You have to!'

The bin men collect it
And sort it through
To make new products
For me and you.

Recycle your waste
And make all things green
To stop all the smog
Which shouldn't be seen.

So you know what you have to do
Recycle those bottles
Bags and tins too!

Lauren Foster (12)
Chipping Campden School, Gloucester

Don't Be Mean, Keep It Clean!

Recycle, recycle
Don't be mean.

Recycle, recycle
Come on, stay green!

Recycle, recycle
It's a very good thing.

Recycle, recycle
You could do it whilst you sing!

Recycle, recycle
You should do it every day.

Recycle, recycle
That's what people say!

Chloe Masters (11)
Chipping Campden School, Gloucester

Where's My Home?

Where is my home?
The wood echoed with a mighty groan
What once was a rainforest, lush and green
Was now nowhere to be seen.

Far away, beyond the stalks,
This is where the woodman walks,
This is where the crime took place,
At a rather alarming pace.

Back at the wood,
The animals had nowhere to go,
Slowly they began to feel rather low,
Soon the forest lay still.

Maddie Higgins (11)
Chipping Campden School, Gloucester

Poverty

The world is great, no matter what,
From the elephants to the little flies that we swat.

But if we wish to keep it that way,
You must stop poverty and polluting
And start recycling and redistributing.

Poverty means not going to the pictures,
No Internet, no TV, no central heating, no chocolate.

Poverty means walking barefoot,
Missing school, no music lessons.

Poverty means no washing,
Rotten food and dying of curable diseases.

James Bartoli-Edwards (11)
Chipping Campden School, Gloucester

Litterbug

L itter scattered everywhere
　Pick up what shouldn't be there
I n the night, beer cans thrown
　All around, but no one knows
T he crisp packets hang from tree to tree
　So just put them in the bin, oh please
T ogether we can stop and clean up
　To make the world a better place
E ven if you think it's wrong
　Just help your Earth and bring it on
R eady to go, let's get our gloves and bags
　And pick up the litter - to save our world!

Sabrina Rew (11)
Chipping Campden School, Gloucester

Why?

My future should be,
A girl walking down the street,
Not scared that someone
Is going to come out and hurt her.

My future should be,
A girl going down to the park,
Not scared that some gang,
Is there waiting to hurt her.

Why is the world like this?
Why do people think they have to do these things?
Why can't the world be happy?

Jordan Mazzina (11)
Chipping Campden School, Gloucester

In A Perfect World

In a perfect world . . .
There would be no teenagers
Killing each other over stupid things
That no one should care about.

No gangs or silly people kidnapping children
Or starving them and killing them
And no more people who don't think of anyone else but themselves.

Instead of us being greedy and wasting all our money
On big houses and expensive cars
We should think of people in Africa
Who are starving to death!

Tyler Megan Barnett (11)
Chipping Campden School, Gloucester

The World In My Eyes

I want a world that is as clean as can be,
For people to run and jump in the sea,
For people to walk in a nice clean park,
To play hide-and-seek until it gets dark,
Laughing and cheering and having fun,
Everything was great up until now,
People started to get greedy and selfish
And then war is all around us,
From street crime to teenage gangs,
It gets worse and now it stands
We need help!

Elliott Routh (11)
Chipping Campden School, Gloucester

Environmentally Friendly, Be It!

E nvironmentally friendly
N ever be mean, be green
V ery many wars are happening, we need to stop them
I n the world, 67% of people are environmentally friendly
R ainforests are home to two thirds of living animals and plants
O h my gosh, war is killing me
N ever let the Earth down by destroying it
M achinery is polluting our world by 50%
E very person who recycles is one of 67% of people
N ever say, 'I can't recycle'
T op of the charts is being environmentally friendly.

Charlotte Creed (11)
Chipping Campden School, Gloucester

Pollution

P ollution is rotten
O il and petrol pollute
L ive or die
L ive on the bright side of life by walking
U sually you can save lives
T rouble and hassle can stop pollution
I am asking you
O nly to help
N othing can stop us!

Robbie Faulkner (11)
Chipping Campden School, Gloucester

Extinction

Every animal has its place in the world around us,
But soon that may be gone,
The lion that roars, the tiger with claws
And the little cheeky monkey,
But soon that may be gone,
The little baby elephant,
The long giraffe,
Please help the animals in our world,
Or soon they may be gone.

Andrea Latham (11)
Chipping Campden School, Gloucester

Reassuring Recycling

R eassuring recycling
E co-friendly all the time
C ome and do your bit
Y ou could make a massive difference
C ould help poverty
L ots of help will make the homeless happy
E nough TV, more eco-friendly!

Grace Dembowicz (11)
Chipping Campden School, Gloucester

Being Homeless

Not everything in the world has a home,
Rabbits were in their burrows before their homes were destroyed,
Foxes are on their way,
But they come to where their homes once were
To find them destroyed,
Not everything has a home
And some animals are homeless,
A tree has been cut down where a squirrel once lived,
Not everything has a home.

Beatrice Saxon (11)
Chipping Campden School, Gloucester

Why?

Why chop down the rainforest
And why pollute the air?
Why increase petrol prices
And why be obsessed with shopping?
Why kill animals for their fur
And what is with this war?
Why are teenagers getting hurt
And why are children going missing?
Why can't we stop this?

Matilda Willson (11)
Chipping Campden School, Gloucester

Litter, Litter And More Litter!

L itter's a bad, bad thing, stop it now
I llness and sickness spreads
T his will kill our poor, poor world
T ry and stop killing our poor old world
E ngland's enemy is litter, please stop
R ubbish and pollution is putting a stop to our world!

Bethany Ellen Walker (11)
Chipping Campden School, Gloucester

69

Pollution

W hat is the point of fighting?
A s it only hurts
R unning into death, it is no good thing, what do you do it for?

I s it to save our world? It is better to be fair and safe
S o don't do war

B e as brave as you can
A s you could get shot
D ie - you don't want to die!

Jac Johnson-Fisher (11)
Chipping Campden School, Gloucester

Trash

A ll the animals everywhere
N o they do not brush their hair
I wish I could be a dog or a cat
M y mum could watch me sit on the mat
A giraffe, camel, donkey and more
L augh like a hyena, I would fall on the floor
S uch a weird thing to dream
  I would not like to be a bull, they're mean!

Verity Copeland (11)
Chipping Campden School, Gloucester

Football And Racism

F ootball is a good game, but there is no need for racism
O ne goal after another, people are being racist
O h why, oh why, are people racist?
T eamwork is the key
B oots fit everyone, no matter where they're from
A ll players come from everywhere
L ook at the teams, aren't they very good?
L istening to this poem might change your heart.

Daniel Mallinson (11)
Chipping Campden School, Gloucester

Litter

L itter
I s making the world dirty
T rash smells
T ogether we can clean it up
E verybody can work together
R ecommend you to put your litter in the bin!

Aaron Evans (12)
Chipping Campden School, Gloucester

Litter

L asting consequences to the land
I ntelligent people take charge
T o create a better planet
T he planet needs help, so
E veryone work together and
R ecycle - it will help the world!

Aaron Smith (12)
Chipping Campden School, Gloucester

Don't Be Mean, Be Green!

Litter, pollution, we need a solution,
Racism, war, these disappoint me more,
We have to change our ways,
Don't leave it for another day!

Tom Price (11)
Chipping Campden School, Gloucester

Nothingness

It hurts,
Every time you drop litter,
It hurts,
Every time you waste paper,
It hurts,
Every time you drop something into a river,
It hurts.

I'm in agony,
Every time you waste electricity,
I'm in agony,
All the while you live in greed,
Why do you hurt me so?

I give you so much,
In return I get pain,
I gave you flowers, birds, animals, the blue sky, colour and fun,
You ruined me!

In return you destroyed my flowers,
Killed my birds and animals,
Polluted the blue sky
And made everything grey and dull.

I gave you everything,
But now you must live without the pleasure,
Look where greed got you,
You live in a world where you wake up and it is silent,
No birds singing, no flowers or colour to be seen,
You wake to the empty sound of nothingness,
To the faraway sound of cars and maybe,
If you listen carefully, you will hear
My cries for help!

But is there hope?
Is there a tongue of light in the sea of darkness?
Is there a flash of colour in the surrounding black nothingness?

Recycle, reuse,
Don't waste, don't pollute,
Whatever you do

Please do not kill me!

Jessica Hughes (12)
Coloma Convent Girls' School, Croydon

What Happened?

I used to smell the fresh flowers
But now all I smell is gas and fumes
From factories that huff and puff
I used to lie in the grass and count hours
But now when I try
The grass is all ruined and tough
What happened?

I used to go and feed the ducks at local ponds
But now they are all dead and upside down
I used to have long walks with my daughter
To talk and bond
But now it's even too dirty
To walk into the town
What happened?

I used to recycle for fun
But now I say, what's the point?
I go around and see people sleeping on the road
Babies crying with their mums
In pain from disease to do with hearts, lungs and joints
What happened?

What happened to the world?
Why is everything wrong?
What happened to the world?
Life is no longer a pretty song
What happened?

Rachel Akinsanya (11)
Coloma Convent Girls' School, Croydon

The Earth Is Dying!

Stop! Look! Think! What have we done?
The Earth is dying and all it needs is someone
Someone kind, someone who can help
Quickly, before the icebergs melt
And flood the land and kill the nation
All because we have got no patience.

Soon the Earth will turn to dust
Then how much is it going to cost?
That's all mankind can think about
Soon, I'm going to scream and shout
Money! That's why we're in this mess
Can we live without the expense?
Time to put it to the test!

What's gone wrong is all our greed
Which causes pollution and not enough animals can breed
Please Lord, save our souls
Then we'll try to stop creating holes
Please Lord, forgive our sins
Then we'll try to put our rubbish in bins.

Think how beautiful the Earth can be
Just believe, then you will see
Global warming would start to go down
Then lovely people and towns won't drown
We can do it, if we work together
Then maybe, the Earth would stay beautiful, forever!

Sandra Ofili (11)
Coloma Convent Girls' School, Croydon

The Earth Will Die

You just sit there
As you're letting me die
Turn the lights off
You're killing me

You just sit there
The fire is burning high
The acid rain is falling
You're killing me

You just sit there
The devastation and destruction
You're silent
You're killing me ╱

You just sit there
The trees are falling to the ground
The echoes are all around
You're killing me

You just sit there
I'm dying
You're getting up, hurry
You're killing me

You're up
Turn the lights off
I am going and I won't come back
You've killed me.

Sophie Jones (12)
Coloma Convent Girls' School, Croydon

The Environment

This world is full of destruction and devastation,
I feel it in my bones,
I hear a cry for help,
I ignore it,
Have I lost their trust?
Where did I go wrong?
They are my prisoners,
A piece of dirt,
I walk along the scarred field,
Seeking lost memories,
All I can smell is rotting flesh,
I choke,
The smoke is coming!
I can't breathe,
I cry for help,
But all that comes is stillness,
Silence,
Greed,
All that is left is a ruin,
Useless,
Dilapidated,
A polluted world,
I close my eyes,
Hoping it's a dream,
My life is a pile of ashes,
But we don't give a damn!

Hannah Morley (12)
Coloma Convent Girls' School, Croydon

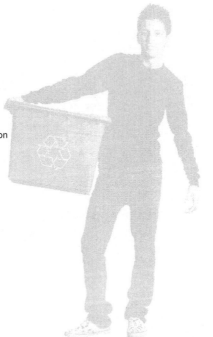

Friends Forever?

'Will you be my friend?'
Said the rubbish to the river,
'No, never!'

'Will you be my friend?'
Said the gum to the street,
'No, never!'

'Will you be my friend?'
Said the pollution to the air,
'No, never!'

'Will you be my friend?'
Said the acid to the rain,
'No, never!'

'Will you be my friend?'
Said the fire to the trees,
'No, never!'

'Will you be my friend?'
Said Death to Life,
'No, never!'

'Will you be my friend?'
Said the Man to the Earth,
'You have one last chance . . .'

Rocio Crispin (12)
Coloma Convent Girls' School, Croydon

The World

T he world used to be a wonderful place
H elp me get it back
E xcuses, excuses; that's all we give when all we need is care

W arning everyone, help me now
O r the world will end up bare
R ebuild the Earth
L ittle and often
D on't ignore, but beware!

Emelia Drury (11)
Coloma Convent Girls' School, Croydon

The Source Of All Evil

'Timber!'
Thump!
That's the sound of trees falling to the desolate ground,
This is due to lumberjacks
Evil creatures, the word 'timber' hanging around their heads
All the trees going to waste!
We might as well just shoot them dead!

Vroom! Vroom!
That's the sound of the rich man's swanky new car!
Cars are the source of all evil!
Putrid pieces of metal bought for their shape,
Colour and speed,
While all the time, it's coughing out toxic fumes!

Whoosh!
That's the sound of water rushing down the sink,
As a toddler brushes their teeth,
Letting water waste away as if it falls from the sky!
We need that stuff, you know!

Now you are aware of what is going on!
It's putrid, sickening, disgusting, vile, nauseous, rotten,
It's . . . the world!

Claudia Merlini (13)
Coloma Convent Girls' School, Croydon

The Earth

You pollute me with your poisonous gas,
You kill my people with fires,
Please give me a new life,
Stop killing,
Please be kind to me,
Please save the forests
And be my friend.

Hannah Foley (11)
Coloma Convent Girls' School, Croydon

What About The Earth?

The Earth is giving us a warning,
But we are not listening.
Thud! A tree falls to the ground,
Crack! There is an earthquake,
But we are still not listening.

Pollution is taking over,
But we are not noticing.
Brum! All our cars are starting,
Puff! Smoke fills the air,
But we are still not noticing.

Nature is dying,
But we are not watching.
Crunch! A flower is stepped on,
Splat! Oil kills animals in the sea,
But we are still not watching.

Ice is melting,
There is litter everywhere,
The ozone layer is being destroyed,
The world is ending,
It is all our fault,
But still, nothing is what we are doing!

Molly McGing (12)
Coloma Convent Girls' School, Croydon

Children Of The Future

They're going to miss the sun,
They're going to miss the moon,
They're going to miss the shining stars
And it's all down to you!

They're going to miss the orchards,
They're going to miss the oaks,
They're going to miss the mighty mountains
And it's all down to you!

They're going to miss the sharks,
They're going to miss the bears,
They're going to miss the enormous elephants
And it's all down to you!

Wash up, take a shower,
Recycle, walk,
Turn off the light,
It's all down to you!

The children of the future,
Will miss these natural sights,
There is enough time to change,
It's all down to you!

Niamh Ingram (12)
Coloma Convent Girls' School, Croydon

Our Planet

I'm walking on my own,
It's actually good fun!
I can watch the birds flying from the trees
And feel the warmth from the sun.

I can't imagine a world,
Where the climate changes weekly,
Where animals are dying every day
And storms don't blow as meekly.

The Earth is changing rapidly,
It's only now I've noticed,
I can smell pollution on every street,
The planet's being slighted.

No more snow on Christmas Day,
Due to temperatures rising,
Forests being chopped down,
Leaving their residents with no hope of surviving.

If that's how the world is going to be,
I think I might just scream!
There is no way I could live like that,
Somewhere equivalent to a toxic stream!

Francesca Pereira (11)
Coloma Convent Girls' School, Croydon

Dying

What is going on in the world?
Where has everything gone?
What is going on in the world?
The warning has finally come.

Grass blades turn to ashes,
Fire and smoke follow silently,
Buildings cause more destruction,
The warning has now come.

Greed has come to those impatient,
They don't appreciate our land,
It's always take, but never give back
The warning is here.

Ice mountains melt,
Acid rain falls,
How can we control it?
The warning will soon pass.

What is going on in the world?
Where has everything gone?
What is going on in the world?
The warning has finally gone!

Nicole Bowler (11)
Coloma Convent Girls' School, Croydon

Stop The Rot And Recycle The Lot!

We see the world as a faraway friend,
He's near and yet so far,
So a hand we must lend.

We must,
Try and try,
To stop making a fuss.

Burning trees,
Why? Why?
What a waste of leaves.

Pollution is so bad,
Stop it now!
Because it makes me mad.

Stop using the car,
Take a bus or a train,
Surely you don't need to go far.

We must rethink,
This world needs us,
So please . . .

Stop the rot and recycle the lot!

Julia Rooke (11)
Coloma Convent Girls' School, Croydon

Oh, What A Lovely World!

Oh, what a lovely world,
All the animals squeaking and squalling,
The best time of the day,
Is the morning.

The rubbish you put on the floor,
Hurts me,
As you drop more and more,
It hurts me.

What you don't know,
Is it's painful
And you think so
It's painful, it really is.

As the rubbish hits the floor,
I think to myself, I can't take anymore,
Stop! Stop! Stop!
We only have one planet
And this time we have got to stop,
Filling it with rubbish,
We can't continue, can we?

Rebecca Humphreys (12)
Coloma Convent Girls' School, Croydon

The Earth

I ask you to care for me,
You litter me.
I give you beautiful trees,
You cut them down.
I give you glittering water,
You throw plastic bottles at me.
I give you clear blue seas,
You drown them in oil.
I give you living creatures,
You exploit them.
I give you life,
What have you given me in return?

Megan Hammond (12)
Coloma Convent Girls' School, Croydon

Have To Help!

Animals are dying,
Elephants are crying,
For help, for help!

Trees are falling,
Squirrels are calling,
For help, for help!

Ice is melting,
Monkeys are sweltering,
Please help, please help!

Earth is suffocating,
TVs are manipulating,
People help, people help!

Dying of hunger,
Too many people younger,
Have to help, have to help!

Oil spilling,
People are willing,
To help, to help!

Heather Lafferty (12)
Coloma Convent Girls' School, Croydon

Our World

The world was a fantastic creation
Green, clean and was the place to be
Until a couple of years ago
When people didn't recycle
And people didn't get on their bicycles
The world was a fantastic creation
Green, clean and was the place to be
Until a couple of years ago
When people drove their cars
And the pollution from them was going to Mars
The world is a fantastic creation
And we need to look after it!

Georgia O'Sullivan (11)
Coloma Convent Girls' School, Croydon

Take Care

What have I done?
I give you clean air
You give me pollution
I give you green grass
You give me dust

I give you clean air
You give me smoke
I give you animals
You give me silence

I give you clear blue skies
You give me pollution
I give you spring waters
You give me acid

I give you bright green trees
You give me dust
I give you nature
You give me destruction.

Oma-Louise Odigboh (12)
Coloma Convent Girls' School, Croydon

A Little Warning!

We had a gift from God
Think about what you're doing to the world
It's time we gave you a little prod
The Earth is choking with poison and pollution,
Help the world and do something worthwhile
Be good, help out, start a revolution,
Devastation is slithering through the silence and stillness
But don't panic; don't fret,
There's still lots you can do!
You can help the environment, I bet
Give us your cans
And maybe some plastic
You'll have many fans!
Just as long as you start recycling!

Maria Nelligan (12)
Coloma Convent Girls' School, Croydon

86

Suffering World, Animals And Lives

The world should be our friend,
A sister, brother or child,
But because of our selfishness,
Too many of us see you as a distant relative.

Animals' populations are plummeting down,
Devastation on their lives and homes,
By destruction and bitter people, bitter minds
And putting silence upon the victims of the rainforest.

Peace and abundance was there,
But now is ashes and venom,
Poisoning and choking the air and animals,
Making them endangered, extinct, forgotten.

Rebuild the ruins, the silence and stillness,
To stop the greed, the cries, the pain
And help the endangered,
Come, act quickly, to stop the extinction of animals
And put peace and life in the wonderful planet we had before.

Emily Quartly (11)
Coloma Convent Girls' School, Croydon

Our Earth

Darkness
Black, deathly darkness
My voice echoes in the stillness of this place
Smoke
Cloudy, suffocating smoke
A burning fire with smouldering ashes
This Earth, an Earth no more
A desolate place
A land of poison, destruction
This place a bitter, toxic, industrial site
A landscape like no other
The germinating darkness covering this land
This is what has been left for us
Now, our Earth.

Laura Brophy (12)
Coloma Convent Girls' School, Croydon

I Give You . . . But You Destroy It All

I give you: the Earth
Love, beauty, peace, nature, happiness: the Earth
Singing birds, blue skies, puffy clouds, coral reefs: the Earth
Amber sunsets, multicoloured rainbows, flowers as bright as suns,
Blue oceans: the Earth
Beautiful butterflies, doves cooing, snow-capped mountains,
Glistening waterfalls: the Earth.

But you destroy it all.

Instead of: beauty, the Earth is ugly
Instead of: flowers, the Earth is a scrubland,
Instead of: blue skies, the Earth is grey,
Instead of: doves cooing, the Earth is silent,
Coral reefs destroyed, rainbows faded,
Nature is replaced by cars,
Amber sunsets are replaced by skyscrapers,
Our beautiful Earth has gone, now we have a skeleton.

Our Earth is dying!

Elizabeth Crilly (12)
Coloma Convent Girls' School, Croydon

What Is The World Coming To?

The world was once a pretty place,
But then everyone started filling it with waste.

All the trees are falling down,
All the leaves are turning brown.

The sky used to be crystal blue,
The birds used to sing and dance as they flew.

Now everyone is driving their cars,
There's so much smoke you can see it from Mars.

Animals are starting to go,
The rivers and streams aren't going to flow.

What is the world coming to?

Charlene Coutinho (12)
Coloma Convent Girls' School, Croydon

Out Of The Window

I looked out of the window
And all I could see
Was some gas-filled air
A chopped down tree

Plastic bags blowing
A litter river flowing
Acid rain falling
A smoky wind blowing

Ashes on the street
Fire smoking
Fumes everywhere
The world is choking

Reuse plastic bags
Don't get in the car
Recycle bottles
A little work goes far!

Anna Garcia (11)
Coloma Convent Girls' School, Croydon

The Dead World

The sky black, the trees bare
Lightning crackling through the sky

The sea roaring with laughter
Watching us all choke to death

The volcanoes erupt, ash falling
Into nothingness, the dark, dark world

Memories of before, green trees
Bright blue skies, candyfloss clouds, it was lovely then

Now it has been changed, been ruined by Man,
Spoilt forever, never the same

This is what it will be like if we don't all work together
To help the Earth and to live forever.

Katie Ross (13)
Coloma Convent Girls' School, Croydon

The Earth

The Earth is now polluted
Every inch is ruined
There isn't a part of it
That deserves to be destroyed

The sky is polluted
With fumes in the sky
This happens every day
It pours from cars

People are littering
But do now know
How much the world is changing
And it is so easy to stop

Now everyone knows
About how we are ruining Earth
So please try to look after it
In all we say and do.

Louise McPheat (12)
Coloma Convent Girls' School, Croydon

The World

The world was once a beautiful, sunny place,
It is now a stormy, dark place.
There used to be birds in the trees, singing,
There are now no birds and a still silence in the air.

The world once had a beautiful rainbow,
It is now a grey, sad sky.
The world was once a land of trees,
It is now a bare surface.

The world once had many animals,
It now has only a few.
The world used to have . . .
Everything!

Emily Findlay (11)
Coloma Convent Girls' School, Croydon

The Environment Still Ruined

The fire still burning,
The fire still flaming,
The ashes are rising,
The rain isn't falling.

The animals still screeching,
The animals are running,
Running, running as far as they can,
They are no longer with us.

The world still moving,
The world still greedy,
People still crying,
The bitterness not dying.

The environment still polluted,
The environment is ruined,
What have we done?
The echoes are still flowing.

Charlotte-Nicole Mamedy (12)
Coloma Convent Girls' School, Croydon

Can We Not See?

If humans had never been
What would Earth be like?
No more fading rainforests?
No more melting ice?

We're too busy working
To take a look around,
Animals, plants, oceans,
Just waiting to be found.

Of course, we'll never see them,
At this rate anyway!
You'll never see Earth's wonders,
Because they're all wasting away.

Stephanie Adaken-Garjah (11)
Coloma Convent Girls' School, Croydon

Fault . . .

Fault . . .
That awful word rumbles on thunder and dances on lightning . . .
Fault . . .
That disgusting word sits on the clouds and cackles with the Devil . . .
Fault . . .
That dreadful word grows in the trees, but is never cut down . . .
Fault . . .
That sinful word flows through the rivers and flies with the wind . . .
Fault . . .
That horrible word is imprinted on our hearts and engraved
in the Earth . . .

Fault . . .
My fault . . .
Your fault . . .
Our fault . . .
But not God's fault . . .
That the Earth is dying a slow, painful and poisoned death . . .

Rachel Limb (12)
Coloma Convent Girls' School, Croydon

Earth Poem

The birds twittering in the great, tall, colourful trees
Or the birds squawking and having to perch on tree stumps?

The sun shining in the blue sky
And shimmering on the crystal-clear sea
Or the sound of lightning crackling near the mucky, polluted water?

The deer roaming on the mountains in the beautiful sunset
Or the deer trying to graze near the horrible quarries?

The children playing in the lush green meadows
And swimming in the lakes
Or the children breathing in the polluted air
And having to swim in the toxic water?

Ella Fernandes-Pinto (11)
Coloma Convent Girls' School, Croydon

Burning

The world is burning,
In fire and smoke.
The world is in ruin
And full of pollution.
The only thing left,
Is the dark silence of the world.
Venom, dust and poison,
Choking the sick people.

They promise no anger,
No destruction, no danger.

They have now deserted this place,
There is no vegetation,
No communication, no explanation.
Like the world has vanished,
Retreated
And left this annihilation.

Jessica Brennan (12)
Coloma Convent Girls' School, Croydon

The Environment

I am the sun
You are the clouds
I am the mountains
You are the quarries
I am the bottle being used again
You are the bottle that has been thrown in the bin.

I am the apple on a tree
You are the chocolate bar
I am the sunshine
You are the thunder
I am healthy
You are sickening.

I care about the environment
You are a litterbug
You are ghastly
The world is falling apart!

Claire Ward (11)
Coloma Convent Girls' School, Croydon

What A Beautiful World

The trees sway in the wind,
The birds sing their morning song,
What a beautiful world!

The children lay on layers of grass,
Hiding between fresh smelling pine trees,
What a beautiful world!

The oceans and seas cover acres of land,
Their salty scent wafts over beaches,
What a beautiful world!

Everyone is cheery, having fun,
Animals wander and explore,
What a beautiful world!

The sun shines, the snow falls,
The weather changes, here and there,
What a beautiful world!

Maria Hickland (12)
Coloma Convent Girls' School, Croydon

You Are Killing Me

All the poisonous gas that swarms the sky
You are suffocating me

All the fire and smoke in the forests
You are burning me

All the rubbish on the streets
You are burying me

All the killing and people dying
You are ruining me

All the devastation for those who have lost their loved ones
You are upsetting me

The cries of children lying awake in pain all night
You are disturbing me

Look after our world
Because you are killing me.

Hannah Pepper (13)
Coloma Convent Girls' School, Croydon

Destruction

Everywhere I turn, there is destruction taking place,
Animals are dying,
Rainforests are being destroyed,
All these things are happening because of us.

What if the world wasn't used as a dump?
What if the world wasn't a suffocating place?
A place of peace,
But instead it is a world of greed.

The world is taken for granted,
It is polluted with our waste
And yet the world still keeps on going,
Even when we have been so cruel to it.

Everywhere I turn, there is destruction taking place,
Dust and ashes
And it's all because of us!

Alessia Marcovecchio (12)
Coloma Convent Girls' School, Croydon

Imagine

Imagine a crystal-clear blue sky
With birds and butterflies gliding by
A sparkling, shimmering, blue, flowing stream
Oh, look around at this beautiful dream
The bluebirds are singing, oh, so sweet
Red cardinal's chorus on the tips of their feet
The sun shines down in golden rays
I shall spend my time here for many happy days
Until the blue sky is torn and a background of grey
Is revealed to the world and hides the rays
The flute-like reeds are torn from the side of the stream
This is the start of a nightmare, no longer a dream
It's crushing itself with blood and with tears
I no longer think that I want to stay here
And I shall cry: 'Oh, what have you done?'
And my life is no longer a happy one.

Jenny Roberts (12)
Coloma Convent Girls' School, Croydon

It Is Dying

The world is dying, everyone knows
The trees are going, going, gone
Pollution is everywhere, the air it is strangling
With the smell, it is dying
It is dying.

The animals are dying, everyone knows
They are becoming endangered
Because of us
We are dropping litter
Which kills them
We want jewellery
So we kill them
We need medicine from them
So we kill them.

But it doesn't have to be like this
Why does it die when it could live?
We could save the trees
By planting more -
Looking after them, like our children
We could save the animals
By feeding them
Cherishing them, like they are ours
Lots of new fish could live
In the river that could be clean
Which it has not been
For a while.

So, the world could be back to where it was before
But we all need to help
Including you and me.

Sophie Isaacs
The Angmering School, Angmering

Pollution

Pollution!
The world suffers from it
Pollution!
Causes ice to melt
Pollution!
Kills off animals
Pollution!
Needs to stop!

P olar bears dying
O h, so bad
L ives of animals going
L eopards, lions, lost
U nder the sea, damaging turtles
T igers are endangered
I ce is melting
O n and on
N eeds to stop!

Engines growl and smoke dances,
Killing animals, oh so sad,
Petrol and fumes poison the air,
We caused diseases between us!

No pollution?
The world full of nature,
No fumes,
No animals endangered,
And people happier!

Emily Catling (12)
The Angmering School, Angmering

The Death Of This World

Bombs dropping everywhere
Poison gases in the air
People lying on the street
They have no food to eat

Lend a hand
Give and take
Save the world
For goodness sake!

People are recycling tins
And putting rubbish in the bins
Helping animals keep their homes
And finding more dinosaur bones

Let the polar bears
Stay on the ice
And make everything
Really nice!

So this title shouldn't be bad
And make everyone very sad
This title should be the love of this world
Not the death of the world

We have a chance
Take it now
Or in 2012
We'll say, 'Ciao!'

Aicha Rakhdoune, Stuart Howman & Emma Calder (13)
The Angmering School, Angmering

A Sudden Impact

Spreading like the morning mist
Pollution consumes the Earth.

A sudden impact
A sudden impact
Hitting at full force
Children crying
Half-dead on mystified streets.

A sudden impact
A sudden impact
Hitting at full force
Abandoned animals
On cold streets
The night is their assassin.

A sudden impact
A sudden impact
Hitting at full force
Murderers waiting to strike
On dark corners
As night falls
What is left for happiness?

A sudden impact
A sudden impact
Hitting at full force!

Harriet Colmer (12)
The Angmering School, Angmering

Stop Pollution

Pollution needs to be minimised
So people should open their eyes
For a solution to stop pollution
Pollution, what a terrible thing
Pollution, makes the world sing
Don't wait for it to get worse
The ozone is about to burst.

Kerry Jennings (12)
The Angmering School, Angmering

101

Untitled

I look at this world,
The one we are living in,
Our atmosphere holds,
Our key to survival.

One blink and you will miss it,
A bird flying past,
A blip of knowledge,
Into our existence.

The gravity that keeps us turning,
Might one day stop
Maybe never to come back.

The world as we know it,
Is going to change,
Another ice age, polar shifts,
Making us freeze or slap on the sun cream.

But we are not a lost cause,
There is something you can do,
Just a little thing,
Change something in your lifestyle
And this will make it better.

Emily Tester (12)
The Angmering School, Angmering

Untitled

The oceans were blue
What did we do?
The grass was green
But now it seems
Pollution has hit
We know what caused it!

Animals are dying
But we're trying
To make it better
Like it's supposed to be!

Chloe Booker
The Angmering School, Angmering

Nature

The grass was green
But now it's brown
Do I live in a dustbin?
Way down, down
There are clouds, there is sky
But in my heart they're not alive
Give to the needy, give to the poor
Help the children that sleep outdoors
Help the animals
Recycle well
Help the dolphins
And you'll live your life well
Animals are dying
But we're still trying
To save the world
From its crying
The ocean was clear
But now it's not
It's become a sewage plot!

Rebecca Collier (13)
The Angmering School, Angmering

Litter Less

We're going to fix it, fix it now!
The sooner we do it, it will be over in a pow!
If we get it cleaned up and cleaned up quick
We won't have to worry about dying
For sooner or later, we'll end up flying
Off this world, because it will blow up
Because of all the energy we use up
So let's use those bins to stop penalties
For the minute you drop litter,
You get a little letter and a £50 fine
The choice is yours, not mine
The future is growing more technical by the day
So let's give up thinking and do it, hooray!

Amber Bryant & Jorjia Nye (12)
The Angmering School, Angmering

103

The Journey Of A River

The river, brown and dull
  As dead as a corpse,
    Never a sound,
      Was crystal clear.

      The river was happy,
     As alive as a person,
    Never silent, amazing,
     Now dead, a flowing emptiness.

Help the river
  And everything around you,
    Stop polluting the air,
      Everything will be perfect.

   Then the river,
  Normal as ever,
    Bright, crystal-blue,
Everyone helping!

Jodie Adams
The Angmering School, Angmering

Look After This World

Stop being a litterbug
And do that recycling
Help the homeless
Change that climate to sunny weather
Help stop the racism
Don't be cruel to animals
And look after them
The world is changing every single day
Stop that pollution
Cut down on the fuel
Stop letting poverty in our world
It's just one simple thing to do
And that's to . . .
Look after this world!

Charlotte Podesta (13)
The Angmering School, Angmering

Generation

Generation is only beginning,
And yet the world is slowly spinning,
The cultures are mixing, don't be shy,
So show your face and soar sky high,

Now climate change is only one
And as the list goes far on,
We might be here to see the day,
Second, third and fourth generations laugh and play.

Calling names is not the way
To treat others, large, great and small
Our country walks could one day
Maybe, be washed away.

Litter should be in the bin,
So give a hand and some love
And respect the community
And the people around it.

Claire Heberlein (12)
The Angmering School, Angmering

If

If
You
Kill a
Tree, you take
The key to life
If you kill an animal
For a body part you're
Killing part of the
World, if you start
To slack, I think
You'll find the
World will
Give you
A slap!

Jazmine Loricci (12)
The Angmering School, Angmering

105

The Greeny Green

The greeny green
Will never be clean
Even if you keep spraying that Mr Sheen
Animals are dying
And flies ain't flying
Pollution enters seas
And where are our greeny green peas?
We are stuck in gales
And we are running out of whales
And that beautiful flower
Has no power
All the litter
Is getting too bitter
As we all know
The mountains are out of snow
We've got global warming
So someone start calling!

Adam Mowbray, Lily Parisi (12) & Tara Moynihan (13)
The Angmering School, Angmering

Time To Act, Do You Care?

Time to act now,
We could save
Lots of species,
Elephants to chimpanzees.

All the birds in the sky,
Well, they could die,
So let's help them fly,
By cutting out polluted air,
But does anyone care?

All our trees,
We could save,
Will be no more,
Do you care?

James Collins
The Angmering School, Angmering

Green, Green Grass

There was green, green grass in the past
There was a light blue sky, never a cloud in the sky
I was surrounded by trees, not a building in sight
I saw wild animals running free
I felt a cool breeze on my face
I heard wolves bashing into each other
I felt the water on my face
I breathed the air of plants.

But nobody will see what I saw
Why?
Because there is no more green, green grass
The skies are filled with pollution, not air
The trees that I saw, are not here anymore
Animals have been killed
Used for food, furniture and fur
No, no more lives.

Matthew Livett (12)
The Angmering School, Angmering

Stop Killing Our Animals

Stop killing our animals, you beasts
And stop eating them in your feasts!
Once our animals were alive, but now are dead
Because you keep chopping off their heads!

You can't like it, all the blood and gore
Especially as it's raw!
So, put down your saw!
And stop killing our bears all the more!

Just stop! Stop! Stop!
All you hunters, just need to go
Or you'll get caught in the flow!
So just stop! Stop! Stop!

Tom Jenner
The Angmering School, Angmering

I Want People To Care

I want people to care
Polluted air
Does anyone care?

I want people to care
No trees
No breeze
Does anyone care?

I want people to care
No more cows
No more milk
Does anyone care?

I want people to care
No more trees
No more life
Does anyone care?

Stefan Coney (12)
The Angmering School, Angmering

Change Now

The world is a cruel place
Put a smile on your face

The world is dying
While we are admiring

It was greener
Now it is meaner

The ocean was blue
Hope it will be again soon

Flowers will bloom
And so will you.

Adele Sami (12)
The Angmering School, Angmering

Untitled

Animals were alive,
But now they're dead.
They said goodnight
And went forever,
Out of our sight.
Trees have leaves,
That fall too soon.
Pollution breeds,
Which makes
The world bleed,
So please, leave it to heal.

Holly Coomber
The Angmering School, Angmering

Why Do We Do It?

We are killing the animals,
We are endangering species,
Why do we do it?

We are polluting the skies,
We are killing the polar bears,
Why do we do it?

We are putting them in peril,
We are killing them all,
Why do we do it?

Alex Jones (12)
The Angmering School, Angmering

109

Environment

Litter in the countryside,
Animals always have to hide,
The river is always green
And the butterflies shall never be seen.

All the animals that are rare,
The butterflies, bees and the honey bear,
It's just like saying,
'I don't care!'

This is not a game,
But recycle all the same,
If not, it is a crime,
So recycle all the time.

All the animals that are rare,
The butterflies, bees and the honey bear,
It's just like saying,
'I don't care!'

We all have what we need,
It doesn't take a minute to plant a seed,
We think it's right,
So turn off your light.

All the animals that are rare,
The butterflies, bees and the honey bear,
It's just like saying,
'I don't care!'

Please help us,
Just take the bus,
Instead of wasting our Earth,
Stop the dirt!

Jordi James Green, Cory & Daniel Spyer
The John Bentley School, Calne

110

Our Life

I am a seal, stranded on ice,
I've been here for days now,
Is this the end of my life?
Where is my mum?
Where is my dad?
Help! Please help me,
I am hungry and scared,
What's happening to me?

I am a polar bear,
As puzzled as can be,
There have been no fish for days,
I am hungry and I am scared,
What's happening to me?

I am a seagull bobbing on the water,
My feathers are dirty
And drenched in oil,
Are you trying to kill me?

Stop! What you are doing!
Please don't do this to us!

Kerry Flynn (11)
The John Bentley School, Calne

Change

Leaves spin towards the ground,
Not anymore.
The river is clean and clear,
Not anymore.
Animals roam freely,
Not anymore.
People play in the snow,
Not anymore.
Polar bears trek across the ice caps,
Not anymore.
This doesn't have to happen,
You can change.

Paige Warren (11)
The John Bentley School, Calne

Untitled

It makes me really angry when we hear about
Endangered animals like
Polar bears dying
Birds that ain't flying
Fish, sharks and dolphins too
Just like animals trapped in a zoo
Wild animals should be left alone
Let's just leave them on their own
Please don't kill all the animals
They're just like us, except for camels
I wonder how polar bears feel
When we try to kill them and have them for a meal?
They get hurt, with lots of dirt
Seagulls covered in oil
We might as well wrap them in soil
All animals are scared when we're around
They don't want to be found
Fish, sharks and dolphins
Don't like to be fished out of the sea
So let all the animals be!

Jordan Cleverley (14)
The John Bentley School, Calne

Environment Poem

E lectricity should be saved
N owhere for animals to live
V andalising the planet
I njuries happening to animals
R ubbish everywhere
O nly people will survive
N ature ruined
M elting ice
E nvironment
N ever use plastic bags
T ragic scenes.

Corrinne Young (11)
The John Bentley School, Calne

112

Environment Poem

Crunch! Go the wrappers under your feet,
From all the foods that we eat,
So do not litter,
To save the world.

Plant the trees,
To keep us going,
To keep alive,
All the bees in their hives.

Drip, drip, drip,
Goes the ice,
Drop, drop, drop,
The polar bears die.

Plant the trees,
To keep us going,
To keep alive,
All the bees in their hives.

Olivia Lauren Mackay (12)
The John Bentley School, Calne

Global Warming And Waste

Please leave their rubbish on the floor,
They don't know how much they're damaging the Earth,
When people put rubbish on the floor,
Little do they know, the world shrinks more and more.

Global warming is the worst thing that can damage the world,
Summer is no longer summer, it feels like winter,
When it's winter, it kinda feels like summer, although it's cold.

Ten years ago, we had summer,
Now it's gone, it will only come back,
If we change how we live,
Not leaving an empty plate,
Not leaving rubbish everywhere.

Stacey Webster
The John Bentley School, Calne

Untitled

Save the world and stop littering,
Stop the pollution and save the seas,
Start cleaning up and stop factories,
Clean it up and we can start again.

Stop dumping oil into the sea,
Stop glaciers melting, make them freeze,
Animals caught in traps,
Turtles eat plastic bags by accident.

Clean it, just clean it,
Clean up the world!

Elliot James Snudden (11)
The John Bentley School, Calne

Mud

The brown ground that keeps the plants green
That holds the trees in their plots,
It can be hard or soft everywhere in the world,
The worms turn it up to make it soft,
30% of the world is covered in it
And 70% is not
People dump rubbish in there,
People get buried in there when they die,
It can also be a beauty bath,
The thing is mud!

Marc Matthews (13)
The John Bentley School, Calne

Climate Change - Haiku

Trees are falling down
We are destroying the world
We need to stop, now!

Emily (12)
The John of Gaunt School, Trowbridge

114

I Swim Alone

I swim alone in the seas,
I swim alone,
You send big fishing boats after me,
I swim alone,
In your nets you snare me,
I panic alone,
You drag me up on board,
I rise alone,
With your knife you saw off my fin,
I cry alone,
You throw me back, finless,
I fall alone,
Without my fin I cannot swim,
I thrash alone,
Without swimming I can't breathe,
I suffocate alone,
You sell my fin for £200,
I am dead alone,
My fin is made into soup,
I am dead alone,
Now you hunt my family too,
I am dead alone,
I am the mighty shark,
Helpless at the bottom of the seas,
A snack for scavengers!

James Ivory (12)
The John of Gaunt School, Trowbridge

All Gone

The flowers,
The trees,
The bees,
All gone . . .

The grass,
The chirping sounds,
The muddy ground,
All gone . . .

The clear blue sky,
The pure snow,
The rivers that flow,
All gone . . .

The clear oceans,
The singing whales,
The country dales,
All gone . . .

The litter,
The TVs,
The MP3s,
They stay!

Rosie Brewer (13)
The John of Gaunt School, Trowbridge

Waste

There is so much waste
It's polluting the Earth
Bottles and cans are just giving birth
We have too much we taste
That on the floor we just paced
Kids should recycle
And so should schools
We have to help them learn the rules
We grow more to help, that's what it's worth
We recycle and we help Earth!

Aimee Ashworth (12)
The John of Gaunt School, Trowbridge

Take Care

Take care not to tread,
On flowers that are already dead.
How dare you suffocate the world!
How dare we chop down trees!
When will all the disasters stop?
When will you let us breathe?
How long until we all forget,
The taste of fresh air?
Explain to kids why animals die,
Why they're no longer there,
People shrug off all the tears,
That our weeping planet cries,
But have you ever even heard
The Earth's aching sighs?
Our dying world
Is breaking our hearts.

One person can make a change,
Stand up and the rest will follow,
But who cares if we don't, who will?
Are you brave enough?

Rose Vinnicombe (13)
The John of Gaunt School, Trowbridge

Our Planet

Our planet is polluted
From our skies to our seas
We don't even know we are doing it
So stop it now, please
We are cutting down animals' habitats
And killing our trees
Will someone give us one last chance
To change and stop this please?
Our planet's climate is changing
From so hot to very cold
What will happen to our planet
Before we all grow old?

Annabel Wood (12)
The John of Gaunt School, Trowbridge

Beautiful Destruction

Beautiful trees,
Beautiful grass,
Stop right now!
They won't always last!

If you see the devastation,
Hope that we will stop,
It shouldn't take that much,
To make you realise!

Stop killing our caring planet,
What has it done to us?
If the planet made us wheeze and cough,
We would change to make it stop,
You do the same,
You make the Earth feel sick!

We need to realise,
We need to make it stop,
Stop killing the planet!
Stop killing the creatures,
That's it, full stop!

Carla Rookley (12)
The John of Gaunt School, Trowbridge

Climate Change!

Stop pollution,
It's a very hard thing,
With all this pollution,
What can we do?
Recycle, recycle,
Everyone says!
But we all ignore,
Whatever is said!
Greenhouse gases
Are just too much!
So stop it now
Before it's too late!

Crystal Morgan (12)
The John of Gaunt School, Trowbridge

118

Help

Where will you live?
You know you told a horrible fib!

You said everything would be OK,
But here we are, standing in an empty world,
The sky is black, not a blue spot to see,
You paid such a huge fee!

Driving cars, burning oil and robbing pensioners,
But are they all crimes?

But we don't need to save the Earth,
Do we?
We need our cars or we won't survive!
Recycling is absolutely impossible,
Or is it?

Walk, ride a bike, or throw
Paper in a different bin
Or use plenty of
Excuses!

Is that a sin?

Olivia Tetik (12)
The John of Gaunt School, Trowbridge

Environment

E very second the world changes
N ow if climate change goes on, nothing will survive
V ery polluted ozone layer will vanish, leaving us exposed to the
sun's harmful rays
I ce caps are melting
R ising sea levels
O ver capital cities a polluted smog grows
N ever has the Earth had a problem as big as this
M any animals are on the brink of extinction
E lephants are being hunted to extinction
N ow it's up to you to save
T he planet.

Ben Pocock (12)
The John of Gaunt School, Trowbridge

Why Is It Happening?

Why is it happening? I will tell you why,
Ice caps are melting, why is that happening?
Black smoke in the sky, why is that happening?
The people on the ground, how is that happening?
Nobody is listening, why is that so?
Everyone thinks it is fine, when it is not
Nobody listens to you and me, they are damaging our world
How is that happening?
Everybody knows!

Why is it happening? Pollution is about
If everybody knows now, why aren't they changing?
I really don't know why they won't change
They don't know how to, why is that so?
They haven't heard, how will they every know?
I will tell them how, how will you change it?
Recycling is the easy option, is that so?
Now everybody knows!

Lucy Newton (12)
The John of Gaunt School, Trowbridge

Wasting Wonderful Things

The Earth's a wonderful place
So many things
So many things
That we don't appreciate
We get all animals
We invent extinction
We get wonderful nature
We destroy it all
We get all different weather
We pollute and change it
We have lovely countries
Ever heard of global warming?
We get all of this
But we need to open our eyes
And see it!

Adele Houkes (12)
The John of Gaunt School, Trowbridge

Just A Beautiful Disaster

Our world is falling apart,
It's going down, according to the chart,
We all must try and do our best,
To help save the world, but can you beat the rest?

If we all do our bit,
We can catch the nit,
Who doesn't put rubbish in the bin
And doesn't recycle their tin!

If you turn off a light,
It won't be so bright
And you'll notice a lowering in your bills,
So soon after then, you'll be off your pills!

So, let's sort it out,
Watch out and about,
Our world is in a state,
We can all help, so quick, tell a mate!

Beth Jones (12)
The John of Gaunt School, Trowbridge

Keep Us Green

The grass is green, the trees are brown,
The sky is blue, the clouds are white,
The people are smiley, animals are happy,
The world is green, the stars are shining,
The plastic bottles are at the recycling site,
The cardboard is in the cardboard bin.

Our world is green, not gone!

The days are getting warmer, the months are getting hotter,
The days are getting darker, the months are getting colder,
The Earth is getting older, nature is getting sadder,
People are getting meaner, animals are getting nicer,
People are fading us away, they are murdering us!

So, don't start on the road they did!

Stephanie Hall (12)
The John of Gaunt School, Trowbridge

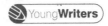
Recycle!

The Earth is all around you,
With lots of clean air,
The world is changing,
But do you really care?

I've been hurt really bad,
Stabbed by a knife,
Do you know how it feels,
To lose your life?

You throw rubbish on me,
I felt the pain,
So I paid you back
And gave you acid rain!

You told me
You filled me with lies
So I'm going to say
Sorry, but goodbye!

Shante Nash (12)
The John of Gaunt School, Trowbridge

What We Do

I am the green grass
And you make machines of brass
I am the birds around
And you are that horrible engine sound
I am the vast, tall forest
And you introduce pests
I am the springs of the mountains
And you put waste into the fountains
I am the animals
And you are the cannibals
I am the last chance
And you don't help
I am the great blue sea
And you destroy me!

Michael Hoare (12)
The John of Gaunt School, Trowbridge

Climate

Look around you,
What do you see?
Because all I see is poverty,
But,
What do we do,
To stop this?
We don't,
We just run away!
Oh well,
What can we do,
If this is all there is?
Will our world end soon?
It will end soon,
If we don't help,
Those who actually try,
Come and help us,
So we do not die!

Michala Blake (12)
The John of Gaunt School, Trowbridge

Climate Change

The Earth is getting hotter and hotter
And it's all due to pollution,
The weather is changing,
To higher temperatures,
Storms are happening,
Hurricanes and tornados,
Sea levels are rising
And glaciers are melting,
But what can we do?

We need to save the planet,
Or else it will burn,
Try and recycle everything you can
And cut down on your electricity,
Which will cut down on your carbon emissions,
Will you do that?

Megan Jones (12)
The John of Gaunt School, Trowbridge

The Earth

I'm fed up with seeing our Earth suffer,
Pollution is changing our weather,
We can reuse plastic bags
And recycle our old, used mags.

The Earth is old and dying,
We all say she's fine, but we're lying,
Turning off electrical things,
The Earth will quietly sing.

Saving energy feels good,
We're decreasing our gas bill,
The Earth conjures up storms and floods,
It is killing the animals and bugs,
She doesn't mean to, but she's angry,
If we see the Earth from her view,
We would also be sad and blue,
The Earth . . .

Manja Suffian-Warr (12)
The John of Gaunt School, Trowbridge

Climate Change

Climate change is getting bad
It's making the Earth really sad
Recycling and reusing is the best way
To help us save the world today

Turn off lights, plant more trees
It's small, but helps the world for you and me
Walk to places, don't use your car
You'll be surprised, places aren't that far!

So, save the world
Reuse your waste
And the world
Will become a better place!

Lauren Fox (12)
The John of Gaunt School, Trowbridge

I Give You A Tree

I give you a tree
You cut it down for paper
I give you animals
You kill them for meat
I give you legs
You drive to work
I give you flowers
You kill them with root killer
I give you one more chance
You ask for one more.

Nathan Hulbert (12)
The John of Gaunt School, Trowbridge

Climate Change

Delightful rivers running by,
Wonderful blueness in the sky,
Admirable trees standing in a row,
Beautiful birds flying low,

But, the real world . . .

Evil waste filling the land,
Awful global warming going to expand,
Terrible tree stumps in the gloom,
Hideous climate change . . . doom!

Jemma Houkes (12)
The John of Gaunt School, Trowbridge

Please Help

Global warming is really bad
Global warming makes people sad

Global warming is really mean
The point I'm making has to be seen!

Global warming is like a polluted dome
Would you like to keep your home?

So, why don't you lend a helping hand
Please join my recycling band!

Amber Coward (13)
The John of Gaunt School, Trowbridge

Recycling

R euse rubbish
E ndangered
C limate change
Y esterday was a better day
C O_2
L ight overuse
I mpure
N ature
G lobal warming!

Sam Horsley (13)
The John of Gaunt School, Trowbridge

Pollution

P eople wander, then people take
O ppress the Earth is what we do
L iving and learning
L oathing our creation
U ntil our ways are finally
T hought through
I n God's eyes we are destroying
O ur eyes cannot see what we are doing
N othing is right!

Rebecca Dewfall (13)
The John of Gaunt School, Trowbridge

What Can We Do?

We throw too much away
Causing pollution by the day
Factories, cars and electricity too
Ruining a future for me and you
But there is always something we can do
To save a future for me and you
Cut down on what we waste
Recycle and play instead!

Scott Pullen (12)
The John of Gaunt School, Trowbridge

Climate

C ars and planes polluting the Earth
L ovely Earth being destroyed by toxic rivers
I f you were to die tomorrow, think of everyone else
M aybe it doesn't matter now, but think of the future
A ll the people around you are recycling
T he world is changing, so should you
E xperience the future, start recycling!

Dan Phillips (13)
The John of Gaunt School, Trowbridge

Young Writers Information

We hope you have enjoyed reading this book - and that you will continue to enjoy it in the coming years.

If you like reading and writing poetry drop us a line, or give us a call, and we'll send you a free information pack.

Alternatively if you would like to order further copies of this book or any of our other titles, then please give us a call or log onto our website at www.youngwriters.co.uk

Young Writers Information
Remus House
Coltsfoot Drive
Peterborough
PE2 9JX
(01733) 890066